# HIS EXCELLENCY THE SPECTRE

# Harold Nicolson's
## Works on International Politics

## SIR ARTHUR NICOLSON, Bart.
### 1st LORD CARNOCK

Sir John Marriott in the *Observer*: "This is one of the books which will be used fifty years hence, as a primary authority for the history of the thirty years or so which preceded the outbreak of the world-war. . . .

"I can only say in a sentence that I should place this book in a short list of *indispensable* authorities for the period it covers. Needless to add that it is brilliantly written."

## PEACEMAKING, 1919

J. L. Hammond (*New Statesman*): "Mr. Nicolson's vivid book is admirable as a sketch of persons and events, and as an analysis, made by an official deep in the problems of the Conference, of the several forces that destroyed the hope of a decent peace. It is a counterpart to Mr. Keynes' famous work."

H. Wilson Harris (*Spectator*): "A brilliant, a discerning, a suggestive and consequently a permanently valuable study. . . . His glimpses of personalities are illuminating. His discussion of a Press-exploited public opinion as a handicap to negotiators is sobering. Mr. Nicolson, as he insists, has not written a history; but he has made a very real contribution to history."

## PUBLIC FACES
### A Novel

*Times Literary Supplement*: "With a rare wit, backed by an inner knowledge of the ways of diplomacy, he has written a racy, humorous and often highly exciting account of the manner in which the Cabinet (in 1939) treated the crisis. This is the substance of Mr. Nicolson's satire, but it does scant justice to his inventive gift and none at all to his skill in portraiture and narrative."

BARON VON HOLSTEIN

# HIS EXCELLENCY THE SPECTRE

## THE LIFE OF FRITZ VON HOLSTEIN

By

JOACHIM VON KÜRENBERG

*Translated by*
E. O. LORIMER

*With an Introduction by*
WICKHAM STEED
*and a frontispiece
in gravure*

CONSTABLE & CO LTD
LONDON

PUBLISHED BY

*Constable and Company Ltd.*

LONDON

.

*Oxford University Press*

BOMBAY CALCUTTA MADRAS

.

*The Macmillan Company*
*of Canada, Limited*

TORONTO

Joachim von Kürenberg : Die Graue Eminenz
Der Lebensroman des Geheimrats Fritz von Holstein
Verlag fur Kulturpolitik G.m.B.H.      BERLIN, 1932.

Whoever first applied to Fritz von Holstein the nickname *Die Graue Eminenz* will certainly have had in mind
the famous Capuchin friar, Père Joseph, who was mentor,
friend and *âme damnée* of Cardinal Richelieu, and was
popularly known as L'Éminence Grise, in contradistinction
to L'Éminence Rouge, his master. The parallel is not
particularly fortunate, for Holstein owned no master save
his own malevolent caprice and lust for power. It is
hoped that the sinister suggestion which the German words
convey, the hint of semi-invisibility and eerie menace, will
equally be evoked by " His Excellency the Spectre."

*First published* 1933

PRINTED IN GREAT BRITAIN BY THE WHITEFRIARS PRESS LTD.
LONDON AND TONBRIDGE

## AUTHOR'S PREFACE

FOR close on forty years Baron Friedrich von Holstein exercised an immeasurable influence on Germany's foreign policy, but to the German people he was completely unknown. He lived the life of a hermit. He went nowhere. He took no public part in anything. He had no use for outward " honours."

Bismarck, Caprivi, Hohenlohe, Bülow, with one voice proclaimed him " indispensable," yet he remains a legend to our generation. His contemporaries admired him, hated, feared him. They nicknamed him " the Mole," " Hyena-Eyes," " His Excellency the Spectre." His policy may have been baleful, the means he used may not always have been fair according to our standards, yet no one can deny his great ability, his outstanding efficiency, his passionate love of country.

" The Life Romance of Fritz von Holstein " is based on historic events or episodes which took place in the circles surrounding the recluse, so selected as to throw his unique personality into relief.

Any attempt to record the whole course of the history that unrolled itself under Holstein's

fingers would fill several bulky volumes and yet remain incomplete.

The author's aim has been, as far as possible, to bring the real man to life, to turn the spotlight on to Holstein's figure so that it may stand out against its background. He has therefore tried to render in seventy snapshots the kaleidoscopic play of historical events, and with the searchlight to illumine the darkness surrounding this best-hated figure of German foreign policy.

His history is the tragic story of a man condemned to work underground because he lacked self-confidence to face the light of day. Holstein remained averse from outward pomp, a lover of negation, a figure of night.

The words of the great Frederick, whose portrait stood ever on his desk, might have been written for him and may serve as his honourable epitaph :

> Titles for fools, to decorate their fame :
> A Great Man needs no title but his name.

# TABLE OF CONTENTS

## I. BISMARCK [1871–1890]

vii

# TABLE OF CONTENTS

viii

# TABLE OF CONTENTS

ix

# TABLE OF CONTENTS

# TABLE OF CONTENTS

xii

# TABLE OF CONTENTS

## V.  OUT OF OFFICE [1906–1909]

# TABLE OF CONTENTS

## EPILOGUE

*The portrait of von Holstein used as
frontispiece is reproduced by kind
permission of Mr. Martin Secker*

# INTRODUCTION

SOME ninety volumes, confidential talks with leading men of the Holstein era, and unpublished letters are cited as the " sources " of Joachim von Kürenberg's work on the famous *Eminence grise* of the German Foreign Office. One hundred and ninety pages tell what the author calls " the life-romance of Privy Councillor Fritz von Holstein." Many thick tomes, he says, could hardly record more than a fragment of German and international history as it was moulded by Holstein's hands. Therefore he has sought to sketch, in outline, seventy pictures to illustrate the life and work of this outstanding yet obscure servant of the German Empire who, time and again, governed it more truly than Bismarck, the Kaiser, Caprivi, Hohenlohe, or Bülow.

If the method of " picturing " be open to question, its efficacy is beyond dispute. Holstein's figure stands out with a clearness which he might have been the first to deplore, for he lived and wrought in a penumbra, and was never more powerful or more dangerous than when wholly hidden from view. Has this clearness been attained at the cost of accuracy ? Is the picture of Imperial Germany, which von Kürenberg—per-

haps unwittingly—presents, true in substance?
Are the " sources," unspecified in detail though
they be, trustworthy enough to warrant the con-
clusions he draws from them? Has he written
history or merely a historical romance? For
sundry episodes in his story no conscientious critic
will go bail. They may be true, but they are " not
proven." Nor is it easy to verify all the alleged
facts. Holstein dead is nearly as elusive as was
Holstein living. I never met him, though I heard
much of him from Sir Valentine Chirol and others
who had known him. German diplomatists who
worked under and feared him were apt to speak
of him with bated breath. Maximilian Harden,
who possessed his confidence and was used by
him, could hardly be brought to mention him
outside the pages of the redoubtable *Zukunft*.
But, having read *Die graue Eminenz* with some
care, I have sought corroboration for its asser-
tions and suggestions in such of the " sources " as
are within my reach. These researches incline me
to look upon von Kürenberg's " pictures " as
truer to life than I expected to find them, and even
to give him credit for truthfulness where proof or
corroboration is lacking.

Here, in outline of an outline, is the Holstein
story. A minor Prussian noble, born in an
ancestral home in the Brandenburg Mark, Baron
Friedrich von Holstein had, as a boy, seen his
father trampled to death by sheep stampeding

from a blazing barn. Later some mishap seems to have made him misanthropic and to have given his nature a " womanish trend." Though not incapacitated for virile pursuits or lacking physical vigour, he never joined a students' corps or held an officer's commission. He was unmarried, and amorous adventures, if any, are unkown. Bismarck seems to have noticed him as a young, shy, awkward and secretive secretary of the St. Petersburg Embassy, and to have judged that he would be useful. Transferred to Paris, where Bismarck's opponent and potential rival, Count Harry von Arnim, was German Ambassador in the early 'seventies, Holstein was chosen by Bismarck to compass Arnim's ruin. Telling Holstein that Arnim was subsidising an anti-Bismarckian journal in Berlin out of the secret service funds allotted to the Paris Embassy, Bismarck demanded that Holstein should get material proofs of Arnim's misfeasance. In fact, Bismarck ordered a subordinate to spy upon his immediate chief. In Bismarck's indictment there were four chief counts : (1) Arnim's intrigues against Thiers and the French Republic ; (2) his anti-Bismarckian view of the Old Catholic question ; (3) his use of official information for financial speculation ; and (4) his misappropriation of State funds to foster a newspaper campaign against Bismarck. Positive evidence in support of these counts was needed, and Holstein was told to get it by fair means or foul.

Holstein bowed and obeyed. According to von Kürenberg he was half-convinced that Arnim must be a rascal whom it would be a patriotic deed to show up, and wholly convinced that Bismarck and the old Kaiser stood for the German fatherland. In Paris he spied on Arnim, took surreptitiously, on carbon paper, a copy of the Ambassador's signature for the misuse of secret funds, and, having furnished Bismarck with this proof, warned Arnim of approaching dismissal, declined to give him satisfaction " on the field of honour," and advised him not to go back to Germany lest a police warrant await him at the frontier. Arnim fought hard. He went to Berlin, was received by the Empress Augusta, sought partisans against Bismarck in the Berlin clubs, and put himself at the head of Bismarck's opponents. Even the old Emperor appeared to be wavering—until Arnim published an anonymous pamphlet against Bismarck on the strength of secret State documents.

Swift to strike, Bismarck set the public prosecutor in motion. Arnim was arrested, tried— with Holstein as king's evidence—and sentenced to nine months' imprisonment. Indignation against Bismarck and his " tool " waxed hot among the Prussian nobility ; and, as a safety-valve, Bismarck allowed Arnim to escape to Switzerland, thinking that Arnim free in exile would be less dangerous than Arnim in a Berlin gaol. But Arnim, in his rage, published another pamphlet, utilising State documents once again, and refusing to give them up on demand. Hence, in 1875, another trial, *in contumaciam*, five years' hard labour, and the juridical epithet of "dishonourable." Four years later, in 1879, the influence of the Empress Augusta and of the Crown Princess Victoria secured for Arnim a safe-conduct so that his trial might be revised before the Imperial court of justice and the perfidy of Bismarck be openly established. Appalled at this prospect and fearing lest Bismarck make of him a scapegoat, Holstein wrote to implore Arnim to stay abroad. Holstein's partisans let Arnim know that a cell in the Brandenburg penitentiary was ready for him. None the less, Arnim stood firm, packed his trunks, and was about to start from Nice when a stroke laid him low. In an hour or two he died, with his gaze on the box that held the anti-Bismarckian papers. On receipt of the news Holstein started for Nice without even a handbag, straight from the Imperial Chancellor's palace. He seized Arnim's trunks, opened them, and burned the incriminating papers, one by one, with his own hands. The awful nightmare was lifted.

Yet something remained—for Bismarck and for Holstein. Year by year the Prussian nobility seemed to hate Bismarck more and more. The old Empress and the Crown Princess shared their feelings. But Bismarck weathered the storm and "took it out of" the Crown Princess in 1888, during her hundred days on the Imperial throne. Holstein, " Arnim's hangman," fared worse. In the club on the Pariser Platz, Count Bredow warned him that his presence might be misunderstood, and led him to the door which, Prussian baron though he was, he would never pass again. Nor would any host or hostess in Berlin society receive him. The boycott was absolute. Bismarck alone protected him. He who distrusted all men felt he held Holstein in the hollow of his hand and could rely on him through thick and thin. No official of the German Foreign Office could vie with Holstein in ability or in capacity for hard work. From 8 a.m. till late at night, year in, year out, he was to be found in his room, next to that of the Foreign Secretary, polishing off masses of reports without ever forgetting a detail, corresponding on his own authority with Ministers and Ambassadors (this privilege Bismarck gave him), entering unannounced the adjoining room of Herbert Bismarck, who was Foreign Secretary, at any hour, and noting carefully the personal weaknesses, talents or shortcomings of every member of the Diplomatic Service from the youngest Secretary to the most experienced Ambassador. Bismarck's answer to the social boycott had been to appoint him " First Councillor of the Political Department of the Foreign Office."

To the Bismarcks, father and son, Holstein became indispensable. Amid their duties and responsibilities they could feel that his sleepless eye was watching over affairs and that nothing would escape him. Little by little the social boycott was mitigated, or would have been had not Holstein boycotted society in his turn. Whenever invitations reached him, even from high quarters, his invariable answer was that he possessed no " gala suit " and could not come. The only forms of social life in which he took pleasure were little suppers or luncheons in a " wine restaurant " —Holstein was a *gourmet* and loved good claret— or parties in the *salon* of Frau von Lebbin, wife of a high official in the Prussian Home Office. But, as appears from the Memoirs of Prince Hohenlohe, the third Imperial Chancellor, and from those of Bülow and others, Holstein's little suppers and luncheons were by no means boycotted by Ambassadors, Ministers and officials who wished to be in his good graces or whom he wished to use ; and from his early days in Berlin he kept in touch with promising or ambitious men like Count Philip Eulenburg, and, later, Bernhard von Bülow.

Holstein seems to have made a point of standing well with " Phili " Eulenburg, long before that gifted, effeminate, and somewhat perverse nobleman had become the intimate friend and unofficial adviser of William II. Holstein's influence presently made Eulenburg Prussian Minister to a South German Court and thereafter German Ambassador in Vienna. He had a hold over

Eulenburg and, according to Kürenberg, over
Bülow also. What it was and how Holstein used
it Kürenberg explains in several passages which
are as explicit as, in the circumstances, they need
be. It has often been suggested that Holstein's
power over Bülow was derived from the posses-
sion of a bundle of love letters which Frau von
(afterwards Princess) Bülow had written to one
of her music masters, and that the casket containing these letters had been acquired by Holstein
from an individual who stole it. Kürenberg gives
a version of this incident that is more creditable
to Holstein. The casket, he says, was stolen
during a party which the Bülows gave in a Berlin
hotel, and Bülow suspected Holstein of the
larceny. He went so far as to charge him with
it, and was promptly challenged to a duel. But
that same morning an impecunious officer, who
had attended the Bülow's party, brought the
casket to Holstein and proposed to sell it to him.
Holstein took the casket, made the officer seal it,
dismissed him summarily, had him expelled from
his regiment, and then handed the casket to
Bülow without more ado.

This story might account in part for Bülow's
subservience to Holstein. Kürenberg suggests,
however, another reason for it. He relates that
one night, when Holstein took refuge from a
downpour in a third-rate Berlin beer-house frequented by sailors, he was astonished to hear, in
what may have been a homosexual rendezvous,

voices that struck him as familiar. They were those of two men, painted and "got up" to look like sailors, who answered to the names of "Krause" and "Hoffmann" respectively. In the smoke and murk of the beerhouse Holstein could not easily distinguish their faces, but he ended by recognising "Krause" as Philip Eulenburg. "Hoffmann's" voice he could not identify until, some years later, he met Bernhard von Bülow once more. At critical moments, when Eulenburg or Bülow showed reluctance to do his bidding, Holstein had but to call them "Krause" or "Hoffmann." It was enough to bring them to heel.

With a finger in every Berlin pie, and informers (willing or unwilling) in every embassy and legation abroad, Holstein was able to guess how the wind was blowing long before a straw stirred. After the death of the old Emperor William, the short reign of the Emperor Frederick, and the advent of William II. in 1888, he knew that Bismarck's end was approaching and resolved not to be crushed in the Iron Chancellor's fall. Subtly, imperceptibly, he passed from the camp of Bismarck into that of the young Emperor, using Eulenburg and other tools as his sponsors. In June, 1887, Bismarck had concluded, for three years, a secret Re-Insurance Treaty with Russia behind the back of Germany's chief ally, Austria-Hungary. This treaty was Bismarck's master-piece. It was designed to prevent the growth of intimacy between Russia and France, and at the same time to forestall the danger of excessive German dependence upon Austria-Hungary. The treaty fell due for renewal in March, 1890, when the young Emperor had been less than two years on the throne. Holstein knew that William II. meant to be his own Chancellor. He knew also that Bismarck often withheld important papers from his Imperial master, marking them either "Not to be put before the Kaiser," or "Not for the Kaiser," or "Revise for the Kaiser." In March, 1890, when Bismarck's relations with the young Emperor were strained for other reasons, and when Count Shuvaloff was already in Berlin on a secret mission from Tsar Alexander III. to negotiate a renewal of the Re-Insurance Treaty with Bismarck and Herbert Bismarck alone, Holstein caused the original treaty to be placed before the Emperor (who was unaware of its existence) and thus brought about the Iron Chancellor's dismissal. The secret treaty was not renewed, and Russia turned towards France. While Herbert Bismarck was still impetuously defending Holstein against suggestions that "the man with the hyena's eyes" was betraying him and his father, Holstein was preparing to plant his dagger between the ribs of Bismarck himself and thus, at one stroke, to take revenge for the indignities he had suffered after the Arnim affair and to ensure for himself a longer lease of power by gaining the favour of William II.

So Bismarck and Herbert his son departed, never to return. When they took leave of the officials in the Foreign Office Holstein was not there. As they drove away Herbert exclaimed, " All were there save the Demon " ; and Bismarck answered slowly, " If fear of the good is demonic, Holstein is a true Demon." How Holstein intrigued and manœuvred in the post-Bismarck era—dominating and presently procuring the dismissal of Bismarck's successor, General von Caprivi ; securing the appointment of Baron Marschall von Bieberstein as Foreign Secretary, only to discard him at the opportune moment ; eliminating from the Kaiser's circle men like General Count Waldersee (who knew too much of Holstein's betrayal of Bismarck), and favouring the advent of Bernhard von Bülow, first as Foreign Secretary and thereafter as Imperial Chancellor—von Kürenberg's " pictures " show in something more than outline. One man only might have been too much for Holstein—Prince Chlodwig Hohenlohe, who, on Holstein's advice, had given up the lord lieutenancy of Alsace-Lorraine in November, 1894, to replace Caprivi as Chancellor. Hohenlohe was a Bavarian grand seigneur, distinguished, upright, experienced and keen of mind. He knew Holstein of old, knew him for what he was, dangerous and irreplaceable, holding him an evil counsellor yet an indispensable wheel in the German diplomatic machine. While Ambassador in Paris—as Hohenlohe's own

Memoirs show—Hohenlohe never visited Berlin without paying his respects to Holstein or supping with him. To his nephew, Count Clemens Schönborn, Hohenlohe said, upon his appointment to the Imperial Chancellorship : " If you hear anything about Holstein in Berlin society—and you will hear much, and much that is unjust—be so good as to take no part in such talk. I have known Holstein for thirty years. I knew him in Paris, I know precisely what he is—but I need him."

Holstein understood that Hohenlohe needed him, though he never felt that he could dominate the third Imperial Chancellor. Secret intrigues and Press attacks left Prince Hohenlohe unruffled. Once, when Holstein made a report to him and asked the Chancellor to sign forthwith a document he had prepared, Hohenlohe observed quietly : " I am Imperial Chancellor, not a councillor of the chancery " ; and Holstein knew he had met his match. From time to time he played his trump card and sent in his resignation, which was invariably declined. Rumours of an impending reconciliation between the Emperor and Bismarck frightened him out of his wits. So he offered to resign lest his " retention of office be one of the obstacles that might impede the fulfilment of His Majesty's wish for a trustful relationship with Prince Bismarck." In reply Hohenlohe reminded Holstein that it was upon his advice that he (Hohenlohe) had accepted the Imperial Chancellorship, a condition being that Holstein would help him. Were Holstein now to withdraw it would be a breach of contract. The visit which Hohenlohe had paid to Bismarck on taking over the Chancellorship was a visit of courtesy— nothing more. There was nothing in it to awaken Holstein's distrust. Holstein was glad to stay. Yet he tendered his resignation again, for the seventh time, when the Kaiser and Hohenlohe went to Friedrichsruh for Bismarck's eightieth birthday. Once again it was declined. The gulf between Berlin and Friedrichsruh was too deep.

Bismarck was not the only cloud on Holstein's horizon. The influence of Count " Phili " Eulenburg upon the Kaiser had increased beyond measure. Day after day Eulenburg was the Kaiser's guest, having immediate access to him while responsible Ministers had to wait and could scarcely get Imperial attention to their reports and proposals. Holstein grew envious—more than envious. As a hard-working official, wrath filled him at the idea that Eulenburg, whom he had sent as Ambassador to Vienna, should be neglecting his duties there in order to play and sing his own songs to the Kaiser and to surround the All-Highest with an unhealthy atmosphere of semi-mystical Byzantinism. What sort of a course would these two unstable and erratic dreamers launch Germany upon ! Worse still, Eulenburg's influence might imperil Holstein himself—Holstein, to whom Eulenburg owed his career.

By chance or design Count Dohna, Eulenburg's deadly foe, called upon Holstein in those days. Dohna and Eulenburg, East Prussian Junkers both, had been "friends in youth." In 1886 Dohna had taken Eulenburg to Court, where Eulenburg's personal charm and artistic gifts had made him a favourite, almost to the exclusion of Dohna. Hence, in his hatred, Dohna informed Holstein that Eulenburg had once been blackmailed to the tune of £3,000 by an attendant in a bathing establishment, ostensibly for proclivities similar to those which Holstein had detected among the "sailors" in the beer-house.

On the morrow, against his wont, Holstein accepted an invitation from Prince Hohenlohe to a "beer evening" in the Chancellor's palace so as to meet Eulenburg among witnesses. Getting Hohenlohe and Eulenburg into a corner, Holstein began to talk of blackmail, political and other; and Eulenburg, who had drunk too freely, promptly told the story of the bathing attendant. Holstein speedily committed every word to paper and took his document next morning to the prefect of police, citing as witnesses Count Dohna, Prince Hohenlohe, and himself. Thus accredited, the story was lodged in the police archives, an official receipt for it being demanded by Holstein. Receipt in hand, Holstein persuaded Hohenlohe that a copy of the story must be placed among the "personal records" of the Foreign Office since " the case " was " well known to the police."

With this rod in pickle, Holstein let Eulenburg feel his power by many a letter and telegram to Vienna. In March, 1897, Eulenburg lost patience to the point of " letting himself go " against Holstein in a private note to the Imperial Chancellor. A prudent and conciliatory answer from Hohenlohe explained that Holstein had been trained in the Bismarckian school and could not accustom himself to an era in which decisions were taken and policy determined elsewhere than in the Imperial Chancellor's palace. " Besides," added Hohenlohe, " Holstein does not know His Majesty and has never come under the softening influence of personal attachment which the kindliness of the High Gentleman inspires."

As an immediate result—a result indicative of Eulenburg's intimacy with the Emperor—His Majesty " announced himself " to luncheon with the Imperial Chancellor and expressed the wish that Holstein might be invited. Holstein declined, saying that he was unwell, and mentioning the nature of his indisposition; whereupon the Kaiser prescribed for Holstein, through Hohenlohe, an old Hohenzollern family remedy. Not until much later, in the Bülow era, did Holstein meet the Emperor. It was on the eve of the Emperor's meeting with Tsar Nicholas of Russia at Björkö in June, 1905, when, after the fall of Delcassé in the Morocco affair—a small masterpiece of Holstein's tactics—the Emperor was determined to conclude an alliance with Russia. Though Holstein had long been anti-Russian, he agreed with the Emperor's ideas on condition that Bülow should accompany the High Gentleman. But, as Bülow was evasive and Holstein was eager to know what was really afoot, he deigned to accept an invitation to luncheon with the Emperor at Bülow's table. Dressed in a shabby frock-coat, Holstein, with Prince and Princess Bülow, awaited the Emperor, who thus met the real director of foreign policy for the first time after a reign of seventeen years. Holstein's appearance impressed him unfavourably. During luncheon the Kaiser spoke of a cordial telegram he had just received from the Tsar, fixing Björkö, in Finnish waters, as their meeting-place, and announced, to Holstein's astonishment, that he would meet the Tsar unaccompanied by the Imperial Chancellor and would take with him only Herr von Tschirschky, a somewhat subordinate representative of the German Foreign Office.

Nevertheless, Holstein hoped, when the Kaiser should speak to him after luncheon, to dissuade his sovereign from the unusual course of leaving the Imperial Chancellor behind. But the Emperor was not minded to accept Holstein as a mentor, and put him off by talking volubly of some excellent duck shooting he had enjoyed in Holstein's part of the Brandenburg Mark. Then, without more ado, the Kaiser took leave of his hosts and departed. From this moment Holstein turned against the Emperor. To talk to him, of all people, of duck shooting ! The fiasco of the Björkö Treaty is well known. Bülow, under Holstein's influence, reduced it to insignificance ; and Tschirschky came in for many a bitter reproach. This very Tschirschky was, however, appointed German Foreign Secretary in January, 1906, against Holstein's will. Over him Holstein had no hold ; and when, as had been his custom with all Foreign Secretaries, he entered Tschirschky's room, unannounced, with a bundle of papers, Tschirschky exclaimed : " Leave the papers here. I will send for you when I want you." The door between Holstein's and Tschirschky's rooms, which had never before been locked, was closed and bolted, and Holstein was told to come round by the passage when he wished to see the Foreign Secretary.

This was the beginning of Holstein's end at the German Foreign Office, though chance rather than design finally brought it on. In April, 1906, the Algeciras Treaty, which closed the Morocco crisis of 1905–06, was signed by the Great Powers. By many Germans this treaty was looked upon as a humiliation ; but Bülow was obliged to defend it in the Reichstag. The veteran Socialist leader Bebel attacked Bülow violently. While he was speaking, Bülow fainted and fell from his chair. He was taken home and was out of action for some weeks. Holstein also had protested against the Algeciras Treaty, mainly because the suggestions of Herr von Radowitz, the German Ambassador in Madrid, had been followed in preference to his own. Six days before the treaty was signed Holstein had tendered, for the eleventh time, his resignation to the Imperial Chancellor. He knew that Bülow would not and could not accept it, and meant to make the punishment of Radowitz a condition of withdrawing it. It lay among the papers on the Imperial Chancellor's table at the time of Bülow's fainting fit. While Bülow was being brought round in the Reichstag and taken home, Holstein rushed to the Imperial Chancellor's palace in order to remove the letter of resignation. In vain he, with the help of servants and office-keepers, searched for it. Princess Bülow had given orders that all official papers on her husband's table should be handed at once to Tschirschky. Without delay Tschirschky sent Holstein's letter of resignation to the Emperor with a recommendation that it be accepted. For once in a way Holstein's luck was out. On being informed that His Majesty had graciously deigned to accept his resignation and had bestowed upon him the brilliants to the Order of the Red Eagle in recognition of his services, giving at the same time the higher distinction of the Black Eagle to Eulenburg, Holstein was convinced that his dismissal was Eulenburg's work. Though bereft of office, he felt himself by no means powerless. On April 29, 1906, the German historian Professor Schiemann, sometimes known as "the Kaiser's pocket spy," told him that, during a visit to Eulenburg's library at Liebenberg Castle, he had found official documents of such importance and in such numbers as he had never before seen outside Government archives, and with them papers that were probably unknown even to the Imperial Chancellor. A dangerous fellow, this Eulenburg!

Therefore on May 1, 1906, Holstein wrote to Eulenburg : " My Phili,—This form of address is no sign of esteem, for nowadays ' Phili ' means nothing good to his contemporaries. Your aim —my removal—pursued through many years, is now at last attained. Besides, the low-down Press attacks upon me respond doubtless to your wishes." The letter went on to cite notes, not lacking in precision, from Holstein's private records upon Eulenburg's character and habits. Eulenburg felt bound to challenge Holstein to a duel. The conditions were serious. The duellists were first to fire at each other with pistols from a distance of only ten paces ; then, if neither was hit, to step forward and continue firing until one or the other fell. Seconds negotiated for days in the hope of effecting a reconciliation. At last Eulenburg declared in writing that he had never worked to bring about Holstein's fall or inspired Press attacks upon him, and Holstein withdrew his insulting letter. Bülow gave his blessing to the reconciliation, and an official minute of the proceedings was made for the Foreign Office archives. But when the archivist wished to put it on the register it was nowhere to be found. A friendly hand had removed it and placed it in Holstein's keeping for future use.

Before the year was out attacks upon Eulenburg began to appear in Maximilian Harden's *Zukunft*. Some of Harden's phrases were characteristic of Holstein's style. One of them said that he (Harden) " would reflect thrice before asserting that any man stood on a footing of intimacy with Prince Eulenburg." Other attacks followed against Eulenburg and his friend General Count Kuno Moltke, commander of the Berlin garrison. Kuno Moltke belonged to the " Round Table " group, whose members, the Kaiser among them, Eulenburg was wont to entertain at Liebenberg Castle. Harden's transparent allusions to their spiritualism, mysticism, and other less desirable tendencies gained point from his comment that these things might matter little if the Imperial Head of the German people were not mixed up in them.

Walter Rathenau and various intermediaries sought to muzzle Harden. But a Court clique, loving Eulenburg little and Kuno Moltke less, was not disposed to let things slide. It compelled Kuno Moltke to take action for libel against Harden. Bülow understood what this meant.

He saw that the attacks upon Moltke and Eulenburg were only a beginning, that Harden's blows were really aimed by Holstein at the Kaiser, and that in this business Bülow himself might be between hammer and anvil. Indeed, Harden's campaign against the Kaiser's " camarilla " found imitators. A journalist named Brand attacked Bülow and linked him with the Moltke-Eulenburg school. Whether Brand was inspired by Holstein does not appear. In any event, the Imperial Chancellor sued Brand for defamation. Before the trial Holstein, who continued to visit Bülow secretly through the garden gate of the Chancellor's palace, found Bülow engaged with two officials of the Foreign Office, in a rehearsal of his speech at the trial. Bülow asked Holstein to be present at it. Holstein prayed to be excused. Brand was condemned to eighteen months' imprisonment.

There remained the Kuno Moltke trial. In the course of it Prince Philip Eulenburg, called to give evidence, was asked to swear that he had never been guilty of sexual perversity. He swore, and Harden promptly took action against him for perjury, producing a Bavarian fisherman as witness besides damning documents from Holstein's archives. The Kaiser and the Crown Prince cast Eulenburg off, as Bülow had long since done. Eulenburg was ruined, and died brokenhearted.

The Kaiser felt his throne tremble beneath him,

all the more during the storm that broke after the famous *Daily Telegraph* interview of October 28, 1908, which moved Bülow—who had negligently passed the interview for publication—to disavow his Imperial master before the Reichstag. The Prussian and East Prussian Conservatives were at their wits' end. Albert Ballin, the Kaiser's "Ocean Jew," telegraphed from Hamburg to urge his Imperial friend not to come there lest anti-monarchical demonstrations take place. Bülow begged the Emperor to stay quietly in Berlin. Bearing Bülow a grudge for having "let him down" in the Reichstag, the Emperor could stand the racket no longer. He announced himself as a visitor to Prince Max Egon Fürstenberg's castle at Donaueschingen, in the Black Forest, where the Austro-Hungarian heir-apparent, the Archduke Francis Ferdinand, was staying, and repaired thither with a brilliant suite. Lavish entertainments were prepared for his amusement. On November 14, 1908, a cabaret was arranged after dinner, the last and chief "number" being the *pas seul* of a ballet-dancer. The dancer was none other than General Dietrich von Hülsen, who, with naked torso and stubby legs, performed amid great applause. At the end he threw a flower to the feet of his Imperial master, tripped backwards, and fell dead near the door. The sky of Germany and of the Court, already clouded by the Kuno Moltke-Eulenburg-*Daily Telegraph* episodes, became heavily overcast.

Holstein did not live to enjoy the fall of the Kaiser whom he hated. He died on May 8, 1909, in his seventy-third year. Before his death and during his last illness he rendered one more disservice to Germany. By communicating the Bismarckian secret Russo-German Re-Insurance Treaty to the Kaiser in March, 1890, he had helped to overthrow Bismarck and to prevent a renewal of the treaty. The Franco-Russian Alliance of the early 'nineties was the natural consequence, as was its sequel—the growing dependence of Germany upon her only trustworthy ally, Austria-Hungary. Of this dependence the Viennese military party had already begun to take advantage after the German Emperor had, by his " brilliant second " telegram at the end of the Algeciras Conference, brought about the removal of the prudent Count Goluchowski from the Austro-Hungarian Foreign Office. The adventurous anti-Serbian policy of his successor, Baron von Aehrenthal, and the annexation of Bosnia-Herzegovina in October, 1908, were based on the reckoning that Germany could not afford to leave Austria-Hungary in the lurch. Aehrenthal reckoned shrewdly. Though Bülow, whom Aehrenthal had scarcely consulted, sulked and was inclined to let Austria-Hungary stew in the juice of her own Bosnian adventure, Holstein so frightened him, by insistence upon the dangers of German isolation, that Bülow came tardily into line with Vienna, Maximilian

Harden being sent to the Austrian capital to deliver a great harangue on " allied loyalty " which the whole German Embassy in Vienna was ordered to hear and to applaud. Throughout the Bosnian annexation crisis of 1908–09 Bülow stood behind Aehrenthal, awaiting a chance to " get level " with his Austrian colleague and rival. The chance came in March, 1909, when Bülow, knowing that Russia had decided not to go to war with Austria-Hungary on behalf of Serbia and Bosnia-Herzegovina, presented an ultimatum to Isvolsky, the Russian Foreign Minister. Thus Bülow, at one stroke, humiliated Russia by obliging her to capitulate to the dictates of Berlin, filched from Aehrenthal's eager brow the wreath of laurel it was fain to wear, and created a position in which no Russian Tsar could afford again to bow to a German or to an Austro-Hungarian threat.

This policy Holstein supported and probably advised. It was his last dying achievement, and it rendered a great European war inevitable whenever serious conflict should arise, or a quarrel be picked, between Vienna and Belgrade. The conflict arose and the quarrel was picked after the assassinations at Sarajevo on June 28, 1914.

If there be one man in modern German history whose memory millions have especial reason to curse, it is surely that of His Excellency Baron Friedrich von Holstein, Privy Councillor and

*Eminence grise* of the German Foreign Office, whose life romance Joachim von Kürenberg's seventy " pictures " caustically yet not untruthfully portray.

WICKHAM STEED.

# TRANSLATOR'S NOTE

IN the rendering of German titles I have ventured in two points to depart from tradition.

The German " Geheimer Rat " or " Geheimrat," though etymologically corresponding to our Privy Councillor, is merely an honourable title carrying no duties with it, and is therefore in fact more nearly the equivalent of our C.B. or C.M.G. It precedes the name as a form of address. I have therefore preferred to retain the German word. The higher grade " Wirklicher Geheimer Rat " (" Real Privy Councillor ") might perhaps fairly be equated with our K.C.B. or K.C.M.G.

" Prinz " and " Prinzessin " in German, as in English, connote royal birth and are used only for members of ruling houses, or of those mediatised houses who, though ceasing to rule after the Congress of Vienna (1815), nevertheless retained the much-valued right of " equality of birth " which permitted them to marry into reigning houses without imperilling the children's right of succession. The head of these princely mediatised houses was frequently entitled "Fürst" (by right of birth), the other male members being Princes.

The title of "Fürst" could however also be bestowed by the sovereign either as a personal or as a hereditary distinction, in which case it corresponded roughly perhaps to our K.G. or a peerage.

For this reason I have translated "Fürst" by "Prince" only when applied to a royal or mediatised royal Prince, and have retained the German title in other cases, hence: Prince Hohenlohe, but Fürst Bismarck, Fürst Bülow, Fürst Eulenburg.

A few brief footnotes have been supplied where an English reader might excusably miss a point. Since all the footnotes are mine, I have not thought it necessary to initial them.

E. O. LORIMER.

# CHIEF ACTORS
# IN THE FOLLOWING DRAMA

THE EMPERORS AND EMPRESSES (KAISERS AND
                KAISERINS)

WILLIAM I.—Died March, 1888, aged 91.

His consort—the Kaiserin Augusta, *née* Princess of
    Weimar.

FREDERICK III.—more familiar as Crown Prince Frederick,
    victor at Königgrätz, Weissenburg, Wörth and Sedan,
    ruled only three months, died June, 1888.

His consort—Kaiserin Victoria, *née* Princess Royal of
    England, eldest daughter of Queen Victoria.

WILLIAM II., "THE KAISER"—born 1859, reigned 1888–
    1918.

His consort—the Kaiserin Auguste Viktoria, *née* Princess
    of Schleswig-Holstein (*v.* note, p. 205).

## THE REST

ARNIM, COUNT HARRY VON—Ambassador in Paris.

BISMARCK, OTTO VON—Fürst, "The Iron Chancellor,"
    creator of the German Empire, dismissed by the
    Kaiser, March, 1890 ("Dropping the Pilot").

His wife—Fürstin Johanna.

BISMARCK, HERBERT VON—eldest son of above. Secretary
    of State for Foreign Affairs under his father.

BISMARCK, WILLIAM VON (BILL)—second son of Otto von
    Bismarck.

BRAMANN—Physician in attendance on the Crown Prince (Emperor) Frederick.

BÜLOW, BERNHARD VON, COUNT—later Fürst, Diplomat: Envoy in Bucharest, Ambassador in Rome, Secretary of State for Foreign Affairs, Imperial Chancellor.

His wife—Donna Maria (" La Contessina "). Divorced wife of Count Dönhoff, daughter of Donna Laura Minghetti (by first husband, Prince Paolo Camporeale).

BÜLOW, HANS VON—Pianist; authority on Beethoven and Brahms. Director of Court Orchestra at Meiningen. First husband of Cosima von Liszt (later Cosima Wagner).

CONTESSINA, LA—v. Bülow, Maria von.

EULENBURG, AUGUST ZU, COUNT—Court Marshal, Master of the Ceremonies, Lord Chamberlain.

EULENBURG, BOTHO ZU—brother of above, Prussian Minister-President.

EULENBURG, FRIEDRICH (FRITZ) ZU—(v. note, p. 4).

EULENBURG, PHILIP ZU, COUNT—later Fürst zu Eulenburg-Hertefeld. Cousin of August and Botho, Ambassador in Munich and Vienna. Intimate friend of Kaiser William II. (" Phili ").

HATZFELD, PAUL—Ambassador in London, friend of Holstein.

HARDEN, MAXIMILIAN—Journalist, né Wittowski, tool of Holstein.

HOHENLOHE, PRINCE CHLODWIG ZU HOHENLOHE-SCHIL-LINGSFÜRST—Imperial Chancellor.

HOHENLOHE, PRINCE ALEXANDER ZU—son of above.

HOLSTEIN, FRIEDRICH (FRITZ) VON, BARON—born 1837, Geheimrat, Excellency, Diplomat: Secretary to Paris

xliv

Embassy, Private Secretary to Bismarck, First Councillor and Permanent Under-Secretary of Foreign Office.

KIDERLEN (-WÄCHTER)—Minister in Bucharest, Secretary of State for Foreign Affairs.

LEBBIN, FRAU HELENE VON, " LENA "—friend of Holstein.

LENA—*v*. LEBBIN.

LUCANUS, FRIEDRICH KARL VON—Chief of Civil Cabinet.

MARSCHALL (VON BIEBERSTEIN), BARON—Secretary of State for Foreign Affairs, Ambassador in Copenhagen, in London.

PHILI—*v*. EULENBURG, PHILIP.

RICHTHOFEN, OSWALD VON, BARON—Secretary of State for Foreign Affairs.

RÖBER, FRAU (RÖBERCHEN)—Housekeeper to Holstein.

TSCHIRSCHKY, HEINRICH LEONHARD VON—Secretary of State for Foreign Affairs.

WALDERSEE, ALFRED VON, COUNT—General.  Chief of General Staff.  General Field Marshall in command of troops in China during Boxer Rising.

WITTOWSKI—*v*. HARDEN.

## CHANCELLORS

| | |
|---|---|
| BISMARCK, 1871–1890 | HOHENLOHE, 1894–1900. |
| CAPRIVI, 1890–1894 | BÜLOW, 1900–1909. |

## SECRETARIES OF STATE FOR FOREIGN AFFAIRS

| | |
|---|---|
| HERBERT BISMARCK, to 1890 | BÜLOW, to 1900 |
| MARSCHALL, to 1897 | RICHTHOFEN, to 1906 |
| | TSCHIRSCHKY, to 1907 |

# I. BISMARCK [1871—1890]

# HIS EXCELLENCY THE SPECTRE

## I

THE deep-set windows of the Schleinitz Palace flung their radiance into the night and cast the shadows of their gilded screens on the Cour de l'Approche, on the flowerbeds of the Rondeau, and now and then on a figure which paced to and fro, halting from time to time to listen to the music. Philip Eulenburg was the first guest to withdraw from the festivities. The Church of the Holy Trinity was striking half-past eleven. There was still time. The Bismarcks never expected anyone before midnight.

Bismarck—and Schleinitz! The two great houses back to back, so near, yet sundered by so profound a gulf; Athens and Sparta! Here was Athens. It was a Serenade of Mozart's they were playing now, if he was not mistaken. He conjured up again the scene he had just quitted: his hostess, Mimi Schleinitz, and her friend, Helmholtz: the whole of cultured Berlin circling round Hochberg, who had taken him aside:

3

" Just think it over, Eulenburg," he had said. " You have genius. You should give your whole time to Music and to Art ! "

How they had understood him, appreciated his music, fêted him ! And now he must go on to the Bismarcks, for his father had insisted on it and was ill-pleased to see his son taken up with " theatricalities." To the Bismarcks—to Sparta !

He recalled his own last letter to young Bernhard von Bülow, his friend :

" Prussian character and Prussian ways are stern and uncompromising. Sensitive natures like yours are of different stuff. I realise already that nothing but love of country will avail to bridge the gulf between my nature and Prussia's."

Slowly, reluctantly, he quitted the friendly house. In front of him stretched the deserted Wilhelmstrasse and the long one-storeyed No. 76. " Uncle Fritz's " * window looked blindly down on him. He would soon be starting work there. " Not everyone can be so interminably hard-working as Uncle Fritz ! He toils like a galley slave ! " A cold shudder ran through him.

" If only I could be an artist. Live just for music and for music only ! " " An artist," the Crown Prince had used the very word. Dared he beg his royal intervention with his father ?

How different the Crown Prince, the hero of Wörth, had seemed to-night—more natural, more

---

* Frederick, Count zu Eulenburg, Minister of the Interior, 1862–78, was a friend and supporter of Bismarck's and uncle to Philip Eulenburg.

human. He had shaken himself free of the usual train of officers, the gold lace and the inevitable pack of aides-de-camp and the ladies-in-waiting of the Crown Princess.

The royal lady herself had smiled on him. He had felt her genuine sympathy as she had murmured confidentially :

" You're happy here, too, Count, and so am I. The Schleinitzes are my oasis in Berlin. This is the only drawing-room where I feel really at home ! "

But he must not disappoint his father's ambitions. With mind made up, he turned into the entrance gate of the Chancellor's Palace. He would go to Sparta and report to Leonidas. A man-servant preceded him across the central hall and announced : " Count Philip of Eulenburg ! "

Nothing but smoke and fug. An old-fashioned lampshade with frills and lace sprouted like a gigantic toadstool out of the mist. The cone of yellowish-red light fell over the bulging glass container down on to the round marble table-top. On the table a ball of wool with a long bone crochet-hook, some patience cards and a work basket were lying. Opposite these a heap of official files on which a pencil rested, here and there some dusty bottles of red Bordeaux with silver-mounted stoppers, a cut-glass St. Louis wine glass and a crumpled copy of the *Norddeutsche Allgemeine*.

There were three places and three people. Near the crochet the silver hair of Fürstin Johanna shimmered in the lamplight, not far from the pencil were seen the slender white fingers of Herbert Bismarck, and behind the bottles, on the black leather sofa, lay stretched the giant form of the master of the house.

The Fürstin's gentle voice was the first to greet the newcomer.

"Well, Eulenburg, where have you come from? Tell us the news."

"I've just been in for a little while at the Schleinitzes'."

"Oh, Eulenburg!" she said reproachfully, as she passed her hand nervously over her little cap: "And you announce it so calmly!"

Eulenburg was unperturbed. "But why not, your Excellency! I heard some glorious music. Rubinstein and Taussig were playing. Niemann and Marianne Brand were singing parts of *Tristan* and, later, Desirée Artôt gave us some Mozart. The Countess was talking of a new Opera House they are thinking of building in Bayreuth; Gustav Richter and Menzel were delighted at the idea."

"You won't find people of that sort in our house. We're not so 'cultured' as all that," rapped out the Chancellor, without raising his eyes from his paper. The piping voice came as a surprise. It contrasted oddly with the cuirassier-like frame.

6

" And what did you do after that ? " pursued his hostess.

" Then I said : ' Now I must be getting off to the Bismarcks'."

" And what did Countess Schleinitz say to that ? "

" She put up her lorgnette and said : ' Not really ? How interesting ! ' "

The Fürstin burst out laughing. " Do you hear that, Otto dear ? Eulenburg is delighted with the Schleinitzes."

" Why not ? " was heard from behind the newspaper. " It's a matter of taste."

At this point Herbert chimed in :

" My dear Phili, you mustn't misunderstand the parents. The Schleinitz man isn't so bad, but the female is perfectly impossible. She's our *bête noire !* And when it comes to the family. . . . They're all divorced and re-married and inter-related to and fro, and divorced again, and, of course, all at loggerheads all the time, and always scrapping ! It's too ghastly ! And Schlein-itz nearly rhymes with ' slime '—and not so far out either ! Was Holstein there by any chance ? "

" Holstein ? " reflected Eulenburg. " Hadn't someone mentioned him ? Yes, of course, Rado-witz—and he had said : ' He was appointed Secretary to the Paris Embassy at Bismarck's wish —a dangerous fellow ! ' "

No ; Eulenburg had never met him.

" He's supposed to be coming to-night,"

added Herbert. " Papa has a great opinion of him."

" So I have," came from the sofa. " Holstein is the most trustworthy man I know, and probably the most gifted and efficient in the service. He ought to make a name for himself ! "

Eulenburg had never known Bismarck praise a subordinate in such unmeasured terms ! His expectation was further heightened when Bismarck junior added :

" You're not only going to get to know an able man, Phili, but a fine character. While you were away in Palestine, Holstein and I became good friends."

The Fürstin dropped her crochet and looked across somewhat anxiously at Herbert :

" You two may say what you like about the fellow, but I can't stand him and his hyena eyes. He's uncanny."

" But, mother, dear . . . " protested Herbert, with some heat, " he can't help his eyes, poor chap. They're threatened with cataract. The oculist has told him straight that he cannot save them. Poor Holstein has got to reckon with that ; in a few years he will go gradually blind."

" That would be a bad look out," muttered Bismarck. " The man is indispensable."

Eulenburg pursued his thoughts—" He must be one man in a thousand, this Holstein."

The Fürstin tried to turn the conversation, and seized on the word " blind."

" Tell me, Eulenburg, is it true that there are just as many lepers and blind people in Palestine nowadays as there used to be in Bible times ? "

" Unfortunately, yes, your Excellency. I can tell you something I saw on my travels that I still shudder to think of. We were beside the Lake of Gennesaret. My people were striking the tents and I went up a hill to get a last view over the lake. Suddenly eight of the most terrifying, revolting figures rushed at me from every side. They were lepers, with their limbs all eaten away and distorted faces that had lost noses, lips, ears and cheeks, devoured by the disease, half-living skulls grinning at me, begging for bakhshísh. I could only draw my revolver to keep them off. Then I flung them my purse and fled, but I can't get the picture of them out of my mind."

" The unhappy creatures ; how terrible ! " sighed the Fürstin. " How eagerly they must have waited for the Saviour ! What a comfort it is, my dear Eulenburg, that we have no lepers in Germany ! "

" Baron von Holstein," announced the footman.

Eulenburg was disappointed : an insignificant-looking man, thirty-five perhaps, in none-too-well-fitting clothes. His awkward movements accentuated the unfavourable impression.

" Not much of the diplomat about him," was Eulenburg's reflection. " And a chap like that in Paris ! "

Holstein took a seat on the leather sofa beside his chief, within the circle of lamplight. His face was sallow and ungroomed. How old-fashioned his watchchain was, while his tie-pin might have come " out of the ark." As the phrase crossed Eulenburg's mind, he remembered how his father used it for everything antediluvian or in bad taste.

The unprecedented happened : the Chancellor poured Holstein out a glass of his Haut Brion. Herbert watched the rite almost with reverence, and, while Fürstin Johanna ostentatiously went on with her crochet, she stooped forward a little to watch the guest from under the lampshade.

" Well, now, Holstein," the Fürst began. " You've come through Munich. What's the news ? Did you call at the Embassy ? "

" No, sir, I didn't. To tell the truth, the Ambassador has no great love for me."

" Never mind. He can't stand me either. But the affection is mutual," laughed the Chancellor.

" And how are things going there ? "

" Liberalism is all the rage, sir. It almost looks as if they made it the fashion just to annoy Berlin."

" I can quite believe it. But the Ministry ought to be careful. Liberalism is liable to take the bit in its teeth and bolt further than its professors intend."

For Holstein this phrase formulated what he himself had always felt. He gave a sketch of the general situation in Munich and closed his account with :

" It's my own belief, sir, that at the moment their motto is ' The Empire's extremity is Bavaria's opportunity.' "

The long pipe emitted a cloud of smoke. The silence was broken only by Tyras, sleeping at his master's feet and hunting in his dreams ; the short snappy barking ceased at once when the lowered pipe administered a gentle reminder.

" You've hit the nail on the head, Holstein. And how's Paris ? "

" Look here, Phili," said Herbert at this point, " let's go and see Lenbach's new portrait of papa. It's out in the conservatory."

Half an hour later Holstein and Philip Eulenburg found themselves out in the street in front of the Chancellor's Palace. Each felt that it would be wise to get to know the other. They went together to Borchardt's. Eulenburg was amazed to find how fastidious his new acquaintance was. This unpretentious-looking man, if no *gourmand*, was a consummate *gourmet*. While they talked politics Holstein interjected :

" You know, Count, there's no beef outside Vienna ! " or " Have you ever drunk Irroy in France when it is just exactly right ? " or " The whole secret of cooking spinach is to mix in a few finely-chopped chestnuts."

His frankness about his passion for the cuisine

was more than balanced by his extreme caution whenever political topics were broached. Eulenburg felt the other's reserve and distrust, but if he was to obey his father's wishes he must think of his career, and it was clear that without Holstein's favour success would soon be impossible. The young lawyer found himself courteously heard even when he talked of music and of art.

"People like that are fairly harmless," Holstein reflected, "but 'Uncle Fritz' and the whole family have to be reckoned with. This young man may be useful some day ; he may help to create an atmosphere or the like," for the Holsteins were immigrants, intruders into the sacred circles of Prussia and the Hohenzollern.

Holstein drank his health. "Here's to our very good friendship, Count !"

"Thank you very much," replied the other, with entire sincerity. "It won't be my fault if we're not friends. If you've ever got the time, and care to look me up, I'll play you some of my own new music." Eulenburg knew no higher token of goodwill to offer.

They walked down the Wilhelmstrasse chatting. The night and its influences had dispelled their inhibitions. They had got as far as the Belle-Alliance Platz. It was 2 a.m. Eulenburg wondered where on earth the other was off to. Borchardt's pet gourmet could not have his lair in this very bourgeois part of the city.

"Good night, Count. Best luck. I live in the

Grossbeerenstrasse. I should very much like to see you to-morrow before I start for Paris if you can manage it. Could we meet in the evening about nine ? As near the Foreign Office as is possible ? "

" Right oh ! Shall we say at Dressel's ? "

" Not there, please. It's too full of *jeunesse isidorée.*"

Eulenburg had to laugh. The man was confoundedly clever.

" Shall we say at Hiller's, then ? "

" Right, to-morrow at Hiller's—or, rather, to-day."

" There's a character for you ! " thought Eulenburg. " A queer fish. I can't make him out. What was it the Chancellor said : ' Holstein will make his name yet.' " And again the old yearning assailed him : " If only I could be an artist. I'll never be successful as a diplomat. I haven't got the right make-up."

He pursued these meditations in a rickety cab as he drove home to the large house his father rented in the Wilhelmstrasse. On the marble steps he turned to pay the driver.

Meantime Holstein was climbing up the modest iron staircase of the great stone block of flats where he had his unpretentious rooms. They possessed only the minimum necessary equipment of a " furnished apartment," but in the corner of the bedroom stood a large iron safe. Out of this he took a new file-cover and quickly

13

but carefully recorded the evening's conversation. He fastened in the sheets and ranged the file along with many others.

"It's just as well; you never know," he sighed, as at last he lay down on his iron bed. "But—stop." He had forgotten something. He lit the candle, got up and took out the file again, and wrote on the cover in large red letters—

"COUNT PHILIP ZU EULENBURG."

## BISMARCK SETS A TASK

BISMARCK at his desk.

"Sit down, Holstein! Now for last night. This young Philip Eulenburg—a clever fellow—a musician to the finger tips—he's got something of his uncle in him, but he's weak, he strives after effect, he gets almost hysterical at times—more than half effeminate—artistic, like Arnim. . . . He might make a useful diplomat some day. But it will take time. You'll want to handle him carefully. He is good-natured, childlike almost, but he's got no backbone. Otherwise tactful and discreet enough. But the main point is to handle him carefully. I have enemies here on every side!"

"I shan't forget, your Excellency."

"I gave you a brief hint yesterday why I had sent for you to Berlin. Arnim is getting too dangerous. I've kept some grip on him up to now, but I feel him slipping through my fingers, and he's working on our Imperial master and trying to stake a claim to my post. Mad, of course! But it's time for me seriously to take a hand. And you're going to help me, Holstein I'll lay the situation frankly before you and I hope you will prove yourself worthy of my confidence."

" You can rely on me completely."

" Right. Well, then, Count Arnim said to me once, after a dinner—he can't carry much wine—' I see a personal enemy in every man senior to me in the service, and I act accordingly. Only I don't let my immediate superior suspect the fact.'

" This was after his wife's death. She was a von Prittwitz, you remember, and she died when they were in Rome. The child's nurse created quite a stir in the Zoological Gardens because he had her got up in his armorial colours—red and gold—when she took the baby out. He is very handsome and a favourite with women, so he had an intrigue on with most of the ladies. He started his amorous education young. When he was only sixteen and still at the Gymnasium * in Stettin, he served his apprenticeship with one of the actresses in a travelling company. They had no orchestra, and he made himself up in actor style with her grease paint and played the piano for them.

" Even before that he had been expelled from the Gymnasium at Köslin because the teaching staff complained about his morals."

" Ye Gods ! " groaned Holstein inwardly. " Why must he pour all this out to me ? "

---

* The German equivalent of the English public school or high school.

He sensed the terrible power exercised by this giant who, for all his greatness, was not above exploiting human weaknesses. He did not foresee that he himself would one day be wounded by such another poisoned arrow.

The Chancellor went on :

"It was at my suggestion that he was made Minister on the 23rd of August last year. This year I had him promoted to be Ambassador, for I hoped, in spite of his failings, to be able to employ him usefully in the service. The new dignity is, however, in his eyes, just a higher point of vantage from which to conspire against me, to oust me, and step into my shoes."

The speaker rose to his feet, visibly excited.

"He writes private letters to the Kaiser, pointing out that the Prussian Royal House is now the oldest in Europe, that the Kaiser is therefore the *doyen* of reigning monarchs and that the duty rests on him—by the grace of God—to watch over and protect the legitimacy and continuity of the other dynasties. My master's emotional nature being what it is, this is a skilfully chosen string to harp on, and if Arnim was His Majesty's sole adviser the attempt to cloud his clear and sober judgment might well have been successful. Arnim's idea of restoring the legitimate monarchy in France is, in my opinion, entirely wrongheaded. In pressing it, Arnim is running directly counter to my policy. Now, I never tolerate any interference with the course of conduct which I have mapped out—Arnim must go!"

At this point Herbert Bismarck's head was thrust in.

"Not yet!" replied his father, and continued: "He writes the Kaiser the most hypocritical and sentimental letters: he is 'anxious about the Empire and about my health' forsooth! While to me he writes lengthy asseverations of his loyalty. I've known him since he was a boy, and know just exactly how far he can be trusted. Did you know, Holstein, that Arnim can even weep to order?"

Holstein didn't know, and thought to himself that it might be a useful accomplishment and not so very wicked. It would at least be better than to be afflicted with Marquis Liénard's risibility. He burst out laughing once at a funeral and had to be turned out of the cemetery. The Chancellor, however, had no inkling of the line the Secretary's wandering thoughts were taking.

"Spener's paper is the last straw. Do you know the rag? Well, I can assure you it's stupid and impertinent; both. And who's behind it? Who finances the bankrupt concern? Why, Arnim, of course. And where does Arnim get the money from? Out of *me*, if you please. From State funds. He actually draws on State funds to intrigue against me, against the first official in the Empire! Seven thousand thalers! Think of it, Holstein, just think of it. Seven thousand

thalers of secret service money, allocated for supporting our policy in France, employed in this way by a German official, one of my own protégés too, to intrigue against me ! It's unheard of ! "
The Chancellor smote a ruler on the desk—
'Unheard of, I say ! ' "

Tyras started in alarm.

" I have four complaints against Arnim : first, his attitude to the French Republic, which is not in tune with my policy and may lead to the fall of Thiers, which would be the very opposite of what I am aiming at ; secondly, the line he takes in the Old Catholic * question ; thirdly, his making use of official information for private speculations on the stock exchange—in which connection I should be grateful if you would ascertain for me who acts as his agent—and, last, but not least, the use of State funds for his anti-Bismarck campaign in the Spener paper. Your job is to get me the data on these four questions so that I can take the necessary steps with the certainty of success. Don't spare yourself and don't fight shy of expense. And, Holstein, one thing more : if you guard my interests—and remember my interests are the interests of His Majesty and of the country—you shall not regret it.

" Herbert is waiting about outside. He wants to talk over some of the details with you. *Bon voyage !* And remember to play *pianissimo* to Arnim's *piano—Pianissimo*, Holstein ! "

* See note, p. 26.

c 2

Holstein was waiting for Eulenburg in a private room at Hiller's. He had decided to throw in his lot with his chief—" Bismarck is the man." He would work in the first place for him, and in the second, of course, for the country and the old Kaiser. " Arnim must be a pretty fair rogue." To get him in the toils would be a patriotic act.

He heard Eulenburg's voice and another, curiously harsh, mingling with it. Eulenburg introduced Roon : *

" So you're off to Paris to-night ? Remember me to Arnim. He's a good chap. Just the sort of Junker type I love ! "

" Roon may be all right in war time," thought Holstein, " but he doesn't seem to be a good judge of men ! Or is Bismarck mistaken ? Taken in perhaps by Arnim's personal enemies or by people jealous of him."

He shook out his napkin and shouted :

" Waiter ! Hors d'œuvres variés ! "

Supper went off merrily. They had seen too much of the world to bore each other.

When they had reached the champagne, Eulenburg began with great solemnity : " Allow me, my dear Baron, to present you with this little volume as a souvenir of the beginning of our acquaintance. Perhaps it will help to pass the time in the train ! "

Holstein expressed his thanks and was manifestly gratified.

* See note, p. 66.

An hour later he was glancing through the pages of the little leather book. It was Baudelaire's *Fleurs du Mal*. On the first page Eulenburg had written :

" Tu fais l'effet d'un beau navire qui prend le large."

The traveller let the book fall. Night was growing darker ; the landscape was rushing backwards with increasing speed. Germany was receding : " Qui prend le large ! "

## 3

## SHEEP AT FONTAINEBLEAU

IT was a beautiful spring day in 1874, and Paris had been lured into the country. Even Holstein had made an excursion to Fontainebleau with the Comte de Bellegarde. They were walking through the glorious Forest, round by the Carrefour du Cèdre to the Carrefour de la Croix-de-Franchard, intending to have supper in the little restaurant there which Holstein had suggested because of its exquisite cuisine.

But they did not get so far.

Between the tree trunks Bellegarde caught sight of some sheep grazing. The animals took fright and fled with short, hasty little bounds. He called Holstein's attention to them. The German turned pale ; the perspiration poured from his forehead ; he fainted.

The Comte ran into the Restaurant Franchard to get help. Gradually Holstein came round.

" Thanks very much, Bellegarde ! You won't be able to understand, even if I explain. One needs to have lived through it. . . . While I was a boy a fire broke out one day in the sheepcote on my father's estate. My father ran in to help. The whole place was full of smoke and he fell unconscious to the ground. The panic-stricken sheep rushed out through the door he had opened, out over his unconscious form, and in their terror— trampled him to death.

" I can never forget. . . . Since that day the sight of a sheep makes me ill."

They turned home in silence. Holstein took three days' sick leave.

## 4

## A DRIVE IN THE BOIS DE BOULOGNE

"YOUR orchid, sir." The footman
handed Count Arnim a flower for his
buttonhole. As the Ambassador went
out he threw some letters in through the open
window of the porter's lodge. He patted the
Hungarians, placed his foot on the groom's open
hand and let himself be swung up on to the box.
One man-servant handed up his grey tall hat,
another his whip. At a short, brisk trot the horses
turned into the Rue de Lille to join in the fashionable promenade from Paris to the Bois.

Holstein watched from the Chancellery.
Lackeys in red and gold were raking the paths.
He couldn't help remembering Bismarck's tale
of the nurse dressed up in red and gold to wheel
the baby out—nor Bismarck's other yarns. He
must be alert. No one in the porter's lodge . . .
the letters. . . . He lost no time in pocketing
them. When he got back to his own room he
carefully turned the key. Only one of the letters
was of any interest. It was addressed to :

"MONSIEUR LE BARON HIRSCH,
"11 Rue Carambacelle, Nice."

Cautiously he prized open the flap of the envelope with a paper-knife. He had in his hands one of the items of evidence that Bismarck wanted. Arnim was carrying on private speculations based on official information. The addressee was his agent.

The envelope was carefully gummed down again. Another letter went to post with Harry Arnim's. It was directed to an accommodation address, for even an Imperial Chancellor cannot be sure that his post is not tampered with. The envelope bore the superscription :

" HERRN MAXIMILIAN KELLER,
" Berlin.   Behrenstrasse 17."

Paris was unanimous : the handsomest man with the handsomest turnout in the Bois de Boulogne that forenoon was Count Harry Arnim. There were no two opinions about it.

## 5

# SKILLED WORK

**B**ISMARCK to Holstein :

"In Spener's paper Arnim insinuates that he, and only he, knows how our struggle with Rome could be carried to a successful conclusion, and that nothing but my devouring ambition prevents a statesman like himself from being called to the helm.

"Neither by word nor sign has he given me a hint of the Great Secret. It consists, no doubt, in the thesis upheld by some individual exponents of Canon Law, that the decrees of the Vatican have radically altered the nature of the Roman Catholic Church. I thought of this expedient myself before it occurred to him, but I don't believe it would be of greater efficacy in ending the quarrel than was the foundation of the Old Catholic Church.* This was better and more obviously justified, both by logic and law, than his proposal that the Prussian Government should sever all connection with the Church of Rome.

---

* When the Vatican issued in 1870 the Bull of Papal Infallibility, recalcitrant Catholics in Germany and Austria organised themselves into the " Old Catholic " Church. They reject the Infallibility of the Pope, the compulsory Confessional and the Celibacy of the Clergy and stand for a Catholicism independent of Rome, for vernacular services and for Communion in both kinds.

" I need not go into the Count's other schemes :
they are all Utopian. Make it your business to
get me the originals of these articles. They are
nothing but attempts to cross me and wreck my
Roman policy. I count it very important to have
them in Arnim's own handwriting if possible."

A few days later an insignificant-looking little
parcel was posted from Paris to Maximilian
Keller in the Behrenstrasse. Holstein was not
inexpert at picking locks.

## 6

# A LITTLE SYMPHONY IN E MINOR

SUPPER at the Arnims' was just over. The guests wandered off in groups to the music room. In the connecting gallery Madame de Lecomte stepped up to Countess Arnim: "You won't be angry with me, Countess, will you, if I am curious enough to ask—What *is* the name of that enchanting dish of scalloped veal? It is a masterpiece of your M. Piccard's."

The lady of the house smiled as she replied:

"The inventor of the dish is Baron von Holstein, the Secretary of our Embassy. Lots of people tell me that this combination of veal and fried egg has become popular among the gourmets of Berlin; they call it ' Schnitzel *à la Holstein !* '"

Arnim and Holstein were standing by the grand piano.

"And there's been nothing further from Berlin?" asked the Ambassador, obviously hoping to hear that he was free to enjoy the evening without official worries.

"Not a thing; I was working in the Chancellery till supper time," replied Holstein, adding, with some diffidence : " Only Spener's paper want to know whether they can count on the thousand thalers your Excellency promised them."

" Of course they can. I'm not in the habit of going back on my word."

Thereupon Holstein held out a pad for his Chief to sign.

" What fund shall we pay it out of, sir ? "

" Whatever you think best, Holstein. Which budget shows a margin ? "

" No. 3, shall we say ? " suggested the Secretary in an undertone.

Arnim signed the chit.

Holstein withdrew. He had the required proof :

" Instruction to pay moneys out of No. 3, which is a State fund, for Arnim's private purposes." The Ambassador had not observed the little leaf of blue carbon paper that underlay the top sheet.

Arnim was unsuspectingly turning over his music ; he was just going to play his " Little Symphony in E minor." A lackey was moving about handing each guest a copy of the score.

The lights went out ; the superb music began, superbly played. And Holstein sat by the fireplace, and by the light of dying embers, to the notes of the Symphony, carefully drafted his despatch, clinching his proof with the carbon copy of the voucher.

Having finished writing, he carefully hid the roll of paper in a tall Chinese vase that stood on the carpet beside him. Arnim had just finished playing.

The light was turned on. Holstein unobtrusively hailed a young subordinate :

" Listen. I must be brief. Over there, in that china vase beside the fireplace, there is a roll of paper. As soon as the lights go out, take it, encypher it and destroy the draft. Take the cypher-message with you to-morrow to Berlin and deliver it into Count Herbert Bismarck's own hand. Only to him personally. . . ."

" Yes, your Excellency ? " and the Secretary hastened to his Chief's side, who had called across to him : " Would you be so kind as to turn over for me, Holstein ? This next *Allegro con brio* bit isn't easy to play."

Again the lights went out. Holstein sat beside Arnim and turned the music, page by page, staring out beyond the piano into the darkness and seeing—Nothing ! The blood throbbed in his temples—*con brio*. At last . . . the closing of a door. The second piece was over.

Holstein went to the buffet and gulped a glass of champagne. Now followed the third and last piece : *furioso !* Count Harry Arnim's Symphony was ended.

## 7

## THE LAST NIGHT IN THE RUE DE LILLE

"WHO can that be driving into the courtyard so late?"

"I beg your pardon, sir," replied the servant, "you mean . . . ?"

Arnim irritably: "Why, somebody has just arrived! Where is Baron Holstein?"

"Only a quarter of an hour ago, sir, the Baron was still in the Chancellery."

"What! At this hour of night? Go down and see whether the Baron is still working, and, if so, ask him to be kind enough to step up."

The Ambassador relapsed into an easy chair. Nervously he passed his long, slender fingers, with their handsome rings, across his eyes as if to banish some unwelcome sight.

Holstein came in.

"I've just heard that you are still at work? Is there such a lot to do?"

"Yes," was the laconic answer.

"Just one question: Were you so very busy, Baron Holstein, that you were unable to accede to my wishes and attend the Orleanists' supper to-night? I had made it plain that I considered it a matter of importance that we should be well represented at the banquet this evening ? "

" I was, in fact, extremely busy, your Excellency, but over and above that I had a hint from Berlin to avoid this anti-Thiers demonstration ! "

Arnim leaned slightly forward :

" Surely I don't understand you aright ? You cannot be accepting independent instructions from Berlin ? And omitting to mention them to me ? It is unprecedented. The Ambassador is accustomed to receive instructions from the Foreign Office and to act accordingly. You appear to be endeavouring to set up a rival Embassy, Baron Holstein ! "

" I am doing no more than my duty, your Excellency."

Arnim leapt to his feet. " I must report your novel interpretation of a Secretary's ' duty ' to Berlin. And I shall be constrained to express the wish that you should be transferred. I fear I must insist on this. All my friends consider you a personal enemy of mine, Baron Holstein. I have always been perfectly open with you, perhaps unduly so. Even now I shall speak candidly. So far I have paid no heed to their warning. I have dismissed it all as pure gossip. But things have become too insistent to be ignored and your attacks have become too open. I must protect myself, especially since it looks as if the Imperial Chancellor's office is kept more fully informed of what goes on in the Rue de Lille than I am. Who is that who has just driven up ? "

During this speech Holstein had kept his eyes firmly fixed on his Chief. It was the steady gaze of the stronger man who knows he has his victim at his mercy :

" The Berlin courier has just arrived."

Arnim showed surprise. " In the middle of the night ? Well, where is he ? "

Holstein was silent.

" Well, where's the post, Baron Holstein ? "

Quietly came the reply in level tones, with a slight emphasis on the last two words. " There are no letters for your Excellency."

" What is the meaning of this ? Who is Ambassador in Paris ? You ? Or I ? "

" The courier of the Imperial Chancellor should be able to give your Excellency an answer on the point. Shall I send for him ? "

" Baron Holstein, if you have betrayed . . . if you have basely shown disloyalty to me . . . you who have owed to me so much of your success . . . if so, you are a Judas, an Iscariot, whom I shall unmask in Berlin. Ye Gods ! Why did I not listen to their warnings ! "

Arnim sank back into his chair.

Holstein had remained standing in the doorway. His voice was stern as he replied :

" I shall revert to these insults later, Count, that is, if you are still in a position to offer satisfaction to a gentleman. As for returning to

Germany, I can only advise you to avoid the risk. They would be bound to arrest you and that would only aggravate matters by discrediting the Imperial Government abroad.

" If I might render you one last service, Count Arnim, I should counsel you to accept the instructions of the Imperial Chancellor and remain in the South of France or in Switzerland, and, further, to abstain from any publication or from conducting propaganda of whatever sort against the person of Fürst Bismarck, which would be equivalent to an attack on His Majesty and on the Empire itself. I am genuinely grieved that it has come to this, Count. And now I must send you up the courier who has come on special service from Berlin."

The Secretary bowed formally towards the broken figure of his Chief, who was twitching convulsively, unable to find words.

Dawn was peeping in through the shutters of the Chancellery. Holstein was seated in a cane chair listening to the sounds in the house without, where doors were banging and trunks were being dragged about.

" He's not attempting to show fight ; that's wise," he reflected.

Steps were heard approaching from the stairs. The courier entered and silently handed over a bunch of keys. Holstein was to conduct the business of the Embassy for a few days as Chargé d'Affaires. He did not underrate the service he had just rendered to the Chancellor. Bismarck would not forget to further his advancement and perhaps some day . . . even. . . . He went on day-dreaming, unaware that the courier had long since retired to rest . . . perhaps some day he would take his seat at the great writing-table on the first floor of No. 76 Wilhelmstrasse and govern—and dictate policies—and lead nations !

Next forenoon three heavily-curtained carriages quitted the German Embassy in the Rue de Lille —and Baron Fritz von Holstein lay unconscious on the floor of his Chancellery. The excitement and emotion of the last few days had brought on one of his old attacks. When the concierge's wife opened the shutters, she found him there. His lips were smiling, his features were those of a man whose sleep has brought him pleasant dreams. Both hands were clutching the keys, and the fingers were working like claws.

## 8

## THE END OF ARNIM

COUNT HARRY ARNIM did not accept
Holstein's advice. He went straight to
Berlin, was received by the Empress
Augusta, raced round the Clubs, attacked Bismarck in the Casino of the Pariser Platz, tried
everywhere to find allies for a campaign against
the Chancellor, and openly put himself at the
head of Bismarck's enemies. At first it looked
as if he were going to be successful. The
Emperor seemed to be hesitating and showing
disapproval of Bismarck's conduct in the matter.

And then . . . at this point . . . his very
success was his undoing. He made an appalling
blunder. He published anonymous attacks on
Bismarck based on confidential documents. Not
even the Empress's favour could save him now.
Bismarck struck through the Crown Prosecutor.
Arrest on his own estate—Trial, with Holstein as
witness for the Crown—Nine months' imprisonment.

Every circle of the nobility was full of angry
resentment against the Chancellor and the man
who was on all sides dubbed his " Tool." To

placate hostile feeling, Bismarck let his enemy take refuge in Switzerland, reflecting too, no doubt, that Arnim at large in Switzerland was not by a long way so dangerous as Arnim in gaol in Berlin.

The Chancellor hoped by this magnanimous gesture to stop the howling of the pack. But the ruined man was so impassioned in his rage and hate, that he flung restraint completely to the winds.

He published a further pamphlet in 1875 in Switzerland " Pro nihilo." This attack was also founded on secret documents. The return of these papers was demanded ; he refused to surrender them. A new trial began which ended with a sentence of five years' penal servitude against the absent delinquent, expressly convicted of " dishonourable conduct." Four years after this, Arnim, with the assistance of Bismarck's two deadly enemies Augusta * and Victoria,† was able to get a safe conduct to Berlin to get his case reopened before the High Court and to expose to the public gaze the lies and machinations of the House of Bismarck.

Holstein could guess what this new trial might entail for him—Bismarck would probably sacrifice him and make a scapegoat of him. In an agony of fear he wrote to Arnim, with a lack of mental

* The Empress William I.
† The Crown Princess (afterwards Empress) Frederick, eldest daughter of the English Queen Victoria.

balance equal to Arnim's own. He tried to scare him into staying away from Germany with elaborate and terrifying prophecies of doom. Holstein's friends also brought pressure to bear on Arnim to dissuade him from this " suicide." Others told him that his cell in the Brandenburg gaol had already been allotted to him. There were anonymous letters in plenty, with exhortations, threats and warnings in rich confusion. In spite of exhaustion, Arnim was determined to go back to Germany and exert himself to the utmost to rend the fabric of falsehood woven round him by the whole pestilential gang of conspirators.

He had done his packing. He had on his overcoat for the journey when he suddenly took ill. He fainted. They got him to bed. His dying glance rested on his trunk : it contained documents damning to the hated Chancellor !

He spoke a few words which were not intelligible. Only one sentence was partly audible :

" . . . With the purple, the Duke also falls."

When Holstein heard the news of Arnim's death he started out, just as he stood, for Nice. His first act was to attach the luggage. Item by item, with his own hands, he consigned everything to the flames. Just a few articles were left to be repacked. That was done ! That nightmare was ended ! The Berlin express was due to leave in an hour or two. He was waiting in his hotel on the Promenade des Anglais—by the fire

—over his Medoc—" Had he done the right thing ?" The question haunted him, and again and again he met it with the invariable answer— " I have done my duty ! . . . . What will posterity say ?" The Medoc was welcome. The last time he had drunk this wine was in St. Petersburg—twenty-one years ago—with Schlözer and Croy and the Ambassador, Bismarck. What was it Bismarck had said about posthumous fame?

" Do you know what, Holstein. . . . This glass of Medoc means more to me than thirty pages in Becker's *Universal History !* "

## 9

## THE MALCONTENTS

THE feud of the nobility against Bismarck reached its climax in the course of the year 1884. The entire body of Junkers met in Pomerania in solemn conclave under the chairmanship of the Marshal of the Nobility, completely ignoring the Chancellor, and celebrated a memorial ceremony for Harry Arnim, which brought together all the disgruntled groups of his relations and set new attacks on foot. The Dyke-graves * of Brandenburg held a gathering in Stendal without even an allusion to the Lord of Schönhausen.† The salons of Berlin persevered in their open hostility to the Bismarcks and won thereby the unqualified approval of the Empress and the Crown Princess. In these days of ostracism Bismarck cultivated the gift which afterwards made him so peculiarly feared : he learned to look through a person as if he were non-existent, reducing him to a state of embarrassment that was annihilating—and never forgotten. This gift was the making of him ; and

* On the Baltic coast, where dykes are necessary to protect lowlying land against the sea, the landlords whose property is involved are organised into associations presided over by Dyke-graves, or Dyke-captains.

† Bismarck's birthplace, in the neighbourhood of Stendal.

those who made way for him felt that " His place is at the top."

Every missile rebounded from the Man of Iron. Holstein was sacrificed. The pack worked off their rage on " Arnim's Executioner." At the Casino in the Pariser Platz a former friend waylaid him in a side room :

" It would be more prudent not to be seen here for the time being—feeling runs rather high—I expect you see yourself . . ."

Then with a smile he conducted the speechless Holstein to the door so that the Club servants might not suspect an incident. So Holstein found himself descending the great stairs again, a few moments after having mounted them. He knew he would never see that hall again.

When he called on Alvensleben he found the frame of the mirror stuck full of all the invitations that Berlin issued in the winter season. None had reached him. Yet Alvensleben was his junior. He heard people talking of a dinner there had been at the Spitzenbergs'. He used to be *persona grata* there. Was it true that people were saying —" If Holstein is going to be there, we shan't come " ?

He had been accustomed often to go for a stroll in the Tiergarten, but now fear of meeting people drove him off to the solitude of the Grunewald, where he could be alone. And there, in the course of many a lonely walk, he steeled himself to that contempt for his fellow-men and that renunciation of their company which clung to him through life.

On one such walk he came across his cousin Goltz out shooting. Holstein spoke in French so that the forester who was in attendance might not understand :

" Pourquoi me tuez-vous ? "

To which the other replied, pointedly ignoring the proffered hand :

" Eh quoi ? Ne demeurez-vous pas de l'autre côté de l'eau ? "

Should he change over ? It was too late. His party was : Bismarck ; his master was : Bismarck ; his future was : Bismarck. Deliberately and wholeheartedly he had sold his soul to Bismarck. Holstein was passionately a German and Bismarck stood for Germany. How great the fellow was ! How petty all the rest !

In this isolation Holstein had only one refuge —the home of Hermann Friedrich Karl von Lebbin, Councillor of the Ministry of the Interior, and his wife, Frau Helene. Only under their wing could he feel certain that no one would talk of the ball yesterday at the Crown Prince's to which the entire Foreign Office was invited—except him. Much loss it was ! In his hate he would conjure up a picture of the simple-minded, elderly Empress, obsessed by a desire to make Unter den Linden a second Weimar, gallantly backed by the low-born courtier Schneider, who talked like an

actor, which indeed he had been. The association
of Holstein's ideas used to run :

" Augusta—lace—amethyst brooch," then
the eternal tale of how she " had been dandled
on Goethe's knee "—it was in a mild way a nightmare. And the others were very little better :
fossilised heroes out of Racine !

Helene von Lebbin was a clever woman, and
her society had a wholesome influence on him.
He told her about his encounter with Goltz and
let her comfort him. As he was walking home to
Grossbeerenstrasse he pondered over what she
had said :

" But you are an autocrat, Fritz. An autocrat who loses faith in himself is doomed ! " Or
again : " Only one person can direct a policy :
the most competent ! And that is you ! " Was
he really ?

The letter which he found on his table awaiting
his return seemed to answer " Yes." It said :

" Baron von Holstein is appointed First Councillor to the Political Department of the Foreign
Office."

This was the Chancellor's retort to those who
had been slighting his private secretary. The two
royal ladies would set their teeth and not relax
their hate of this all-too-powerful subject. And
the rage of the Arnim party would swell this hate,
for they would feel this appointment as a personal
insult to themselves.

43

All these things he knew.

At moments like these he would take down Wilhelm von Humboldt, whose letters always lay beside his bed, and turn up the passage: "It matters less what fate overtakes a man than how he bears it."

## 10

# FROM GROSSBEERENSTRASSE
## TO WILHELMSTRASSE

EVERY morning sharp at half past seven the new Geheimrat von Holstein would leave his house. His neighbours in this part of the city were humble folk, mostly artisans or petty tradesmen. They knew him well and would set their watches by him.

Passing the Barracks of the Dragoon Guards he would always take the same route, across the Belle-Alliance Platz and down the whole length of the Wilhelmstrasse. The flower-women and newsvendors would hail him one after another in their dialect, "Yood morning, Herr Yeheimrat." They liked to waylay him, for he would answer their greeting and buy something—a very friendly gentleman. They knew him a long way off; always dressed in black, the thick white beard well groomed, the hooked nose, the sharp spectacles, the serious, refined face.

The little room on the ground floor of No. 76, which served as his private office, was just by the entrance door on the right. He always unlocked it himself. It looked a dismal sort of place with its mahogany-coloured carpet that had once been red. There was a minimum of furniture : a large desk and chair, several shelves with files and portfolios, a row of Gotha Almanacks and one armchair. In one corner a curtain concealed an iron basin-stand complete. The sole human touch was the red shade on the lamp, a present from Frau Helene to protect his eyes. In this room he would work for full twelve hours on end, unless summoned now and then to the Chancellor. At meetings of his colleagues he would nearly always contrive to let someone else take his place.

The messengers who used to go to and fro with papers were in the habit of knocking softly and bowing, even when the Councillor was behind his curtain. They were all afraid of him. The best messengers were always told off to wait on him—the Geheimrat was not an easy man.

He worked slowly. The increasing cataract made reading laborious. But what he once read was his for life. If he ever added a note to the files in writing—a thing he avoided as far as possible—it was always thoroughly thought out, considered and weighed from every point of view.

No one wilfully disturbed him in his office, and anyone who received a summons thither obeyed it with misgiving, for he was believed omniscient and known to be impossible to hoodwink. People's incompetent protégés, however high-sounding their names, were a nightmare to him. He persecuted the superficial with his logic and his insistence, till they either mended their ways or took themselves off. His juniors shook in their shoes. The story went that if once he began to drum with his fingers on the table you were done for, there was nothing for it but to do a bolt. It was common knowledge that he was *persona grata* with the Chancellor, who had been often heard to say : " Holstein is splendid. I owe him a lot of stimulus and many a useful warning, many valuable ideas and wise counsels. He is the best of my colleagues. You can learn an immense amount from him." Or again : " Holstein is so thorough, he has no use for externals or visible honours. Nothing but real power appeals to him."

He was destined to work for twenty-five years at that same desk, to watch Imperial Chancellors come and go, Foreign Secretaries relieve each other, Ministers and Ambassadors follow each other in endless succession. He alone remained, the immovable axis of ever-changing cabinets. Each one took him over from its predecessor as " *chose impayable.*" The miracle was that he was content always to cling to the same post, though outward trifles might be added, decorations and titles, and finally the diamond star of the Red Eagle. By degrees he became a legend. He was never seen, but was felt in every sphere. That was the uncanny thing about him. And the longer he remained in office the more firmly he entrenched himself.

Chancellors and Foreign Secretaries became dependent on him. They exploited his savage lust for work; he did everything for them: drafted their reports to the Emperor, speeches, despatches, letters, memoranda, conversations. The attachés began to whisper, " He must have Jewish blood in him." No one was able to keep pace. His amazing memory made him a walking card-index. The Registrar in charge of the Archives maintained on one occasion that a certain document which was wanted had never been there. Holstein continued to clamour for it, and finally, when it was not forthcoming, grew most insulting. The Registrar complained in high dudgeon to the Chancellor, who had the records searched : the document was found.

There was nothing Holstein did not know. He knew all the wives of the Diplomatic Corps and just how big their dowry was, and when it was a question of filling a post abroad he tolerated no humbug. When he leaned forward over his desk and turned over sheet after sheet on the files, he looked like a mole, and as " The Mole " he was known in the office. Work was his passion and his hobby. He was never happy save at work. People looked on in dismay. He was absolutely inaccessible. He used to work right through till 9 o'clock at night except for a pause of half an hour in the middle of the day, when a light lunch was sent over to him from the Hotel de Rome. When he finally left and locked his office, there was no fear of meeting any of his colleagues in the passage.

Down the quiet Behrenstrasse he walked to a side entrance of Borchardt, Französische Strasse, No. 48. Here a private room was always kept for him. His instructions for the kitchen were as exact and careful as the orders he issued in the office. He brought expert criticism to bear on every dish, and the chef and the head waiter went as much in terror of their lives as the junior attachés over in the Wilhelmstrasse.

The former gave him the nickname " Maître de la Cuisine," the latter " Master of the Witches' Kitchen." His favourite wines were the red wines of Bordeaux and the Rheingau, but he also had a liking for French Champagne and Roederer Carte Blanche.

Towards midnight he would order his cab. The news flew from waiter to waiter—" He's off." Other guests were tactfully delayed a moment so that he might pass out, through the front door this time. He preferred not to be seen.

" Good night, sir," says the hall porter.

Holstein has forbidden him to say " Herr Baron."

No one should know who he was, nor the fact that he was here.

The cab rumbled slowly down the whole length

of the Friedrichſtrasse. The cabbies knew the "Herr Yeheimrat" well. It was a point of honour not to have to ask the address. Next morning the inhabitants of the Grossbeerenſtrasse were able again to set their clocks.

## IN VARZIN

THE Triple Alliance was in the making. Bismarck was hesitating : should he aim at binding Russia more closely to Germany—or at conciliating England ? Holstein was overwhelmed with work. The Chancellor was away in Varzin.* Holstein was finding his work fragmentary and interrupted. He wrote at this time to his friend Hatzfeld and complained of the shiftiness of Italy. He recalled a secret rendezvous that he had had in Florence with Giuseppe Manzini in the autumn of 1872 under the arch of a bridge over the Arno, when the Italian had said :

" The new Italy will not feel bound to suppose that her neighbours share her ideals. She will set soberly about her only task : to make Italy as great and as powerful as possible, be the means what they may."

And what about Austria ? That would involve an anti-Russian policy. Bismarck was a conjurer with five balls in the air at once.

A telegram from Varzin broke into the routine

---

* The estate in Pomerania which Bismarck purchased with a grant of money voted to him by the Landtag in 1867, after the creation of the North German Confederation.

of Holstein's work. The favoured colleague was for the first time confronted with a message of the Chancellor's the inner meaning of which he failed to grasp. He was to come to Varzin. Was he to be flung to the opposition? The journey looked suspicious.

Between Berlin and Schlawe he had time enough to speculate. "Wangerin," cried the guard. That was where the Zitzewitz lived. "Labes," the home of the Dewitz clique. "Zanow," Arnim's place. Ye Gods—not that name! He called up a vision of the well-tailored man in the Rue de Lille: "Iscariot!" he had said. Was this ghost to dog him through life? The landscape was rushing by: lonely, immense, like the great man whose roots were in its soil, who now was calling.

The shabby carriage was waiting at Schlawe and Count Bill was at the station to meet him. Holstein was surprised at the change in his demeanour. He had always felt William Bismarck an influence hostile to himself. It was alarming to find him so very friendly. The carriage turned into the Varziner Allee, described a half circle round the centre grass plot, and halted before the flight of steps. His hostess hurried to meet him.

"Ah, Holstein, there you are! You are more than welcome. You are our only hope."

Count Bill took charge of the guest and dragged him into the dining-room.

There was Bismarck. Holstein had often seen him sitting thus, but yet he felt alarm. Silence.

It would have been impossible to conceive more tasteless furniture and furnishings, with cheap cretonnes over the chairs, the lot possibly from some general suppliers in Stolp. "People who think too much about their furniture, never bother about their food," Bismarck had once said. He certainly did the opposite. On the long table stood an enormous cheese the size of a small cart wheel, beside it honey in the comb, cold cutlets, mushrooms and plover's eggs in salt, sausages as long as your arm, a huge block of butter, Bordeaux, beer, Champagne, between all of which were dotted vases of flowers, candlesticks, fly screens and Dresden china monstrosities.

"He must at least get enough to eat at home," thought Holstein, remembering Bismarck's standing grievance that he was always half-starved at Court. "Everything connected with the man is herculean—even his appetite."

The candlelight flickered on the Chancellor's face. Was it the reflection of the light or the waxen colour of the face that produced so ghostly an effect? The Baron had never seen him quite like this before. The silence got on his nerves.

"Your Excellency . . ."

"Don't call me Excellency, Holstein. Say 'you hapless father!'"

"Thank Heaven he's only playing at King Lear, or one of the Meiningen actors" reflected

Holstein, much relieved that the trouble was merely some domestic one.

" Yes, I am an unhappy man ! What do I care about this confounded Empire we have created, if my own happiness is forfeit ! What have I striven for all these long years but the welfare of my house ! The idiots may call me a major domo if they like. In one respect, and only one, they are justified enough. I am not the descendant of great ancestors ; I am the ancestor and I want to lay the foundations of a great house. And Herbert comes along with this marriage of his which stultifies all I have been toiling for. Holstein, not a creature but yourself knows all the base slanders those intriguers, Schleinitz, Loë and the rest have invented. You and I, we have suffered together. You won't desert me now ? Save me from this woman ! " *

Silence. After a pause :

" Holstein, just think of her at my dinner table. I shall go off my head if we can't stop this marriage. She poses as a Protestant, if you please ! No sacrifice is too great for my would-be daughter-in-law. This Circe has contrived to compromise Herbert so deeply that he fancies he is bound to marry her as soon as she is divorced. I don't see why I should be bluffed into an even bigger blunder than my poor boy. He apparently loves the woman, and hadn't the grit to refuse

---

* Herbert's lady love was Elizabeth, Fürstin Carolath (*née* Hatzfeld-Trachenberg). She had two sisters, married respectively to von Loë and to von Schleinitz.

her and say " No " in time.  But I shall go to
Venice if necessary and see her myself.  She must
have something aristocratic about her.  I want you
to use your influence on Herbert, Holstein.  What
can a father refuse you when the happiness of his
first-born is at stake ? "

A bottle of old Mouton was standing between
them.  The host poured his guest out a glass.
Holstein fully realised that it was the biggest thing
his Chief had to offer.  This vintage was sacred.
It was offered to no one.  Possibly if Johanna or
one of the children had been at death's door . . .

" Now, look," said the Chancellor, in his
normal voice, " if you pour out Bordeaux thus,
from some little height, it mixes with the air.
That stimulates its bouquet ; it tastes just twice as
good.  It's a crime that so few people understand
it properly."  After a long draught :  " Herbert
has got it into his head that it would be dishonourable of him not to marry this Fürstin of
his.  You must talk him out of it.  Then that
fellow Loë with his challenge added the last straw.
You know how cold-blooded these people are.
You are my son's best friend.  You have suffered
under the base attacks of this despicable gang
yourself.  You won't see him delivered over to
our enemies ? "

Questioningly Bismarck looked out from under
his bushy eyebrows.  Hypnotised by his glance,
Holstein rose and went thoughtfully upstairs to
Herbert's room.

The Chancellor could go off to bed with an easy mind. He knew that all would now be well. For when Holstein hated, you could rely on him. He would be off next morning by the first train so as not to be longer away from his desk than could be helped, but before he left he would have dictated the vital letter to Herbert, and for safety he would have taken it, to see to its despatch himself. Which was precisely what happened. A weight had rolled off Fürstin Johanna's heart.

" Come along, Otto dear," she said. " Let's go to bed ! What a comfort it is to have Fritz."

## 12

## AT "THE FLEET"

THE cabs were rattling along over the wet pavement of Flottwellstrasse. The drivers had drawn their white tall hats well down over their faces and only shook their heads wearily when a passer-by hailed them. In such weather not a cab was disengaged. Holstein saw that he would be wet to the skin if he hung about, so he stepped into a beershop such as used to be seen at every street corner in the centre of the city. Through the noise of voices and the reek of smoke, he pushed his way to a corner where he could kill time behind his *Vossische Zeitung*. Suddenly he heard the sound of a familiar voice. He quickly pulled the curtain aside and saw a couple of sailors whose faces he was able to distinguish in the dim light of the overhead lamp ; they were painted up. Holstein took up the greasy bill of fare which strongly recommended its two " special " dishes for the day : rissoles and trotters. At the top of the card stood the name of the establishment—" The Fleet."

Again he heard the familiar voices and caught the name " Krause," and in the light of the lamp he identified the so-called Krause as Philip Eulenburg. Was he here by accident? And whose was that other voice? He racked his brains. It was tantalisingly familiar, but he could not at the moment put a name to it. The false name he heard, and noted—"Hoffmann." He knew who Krause was, but who was Hoffmann?

On that night of October in the year 1886 a new sheet was added to a certain file in the trusty safe in the Grossbeerenstrasse. It was the first nail in the coffin of Philip Eulenburg's reputation.

## 13

## THE EMPEROR'S BIRTHDAY

IT was the custom that on the occasion of
the Emperor's birthday the highest official
of the Empire should give a banquet to the
chief officers of State and to the Foreign Embassies and Legations.

Naturally, the Chancellor's right hand, Holstein,
received an invitation. His Chief was favoured
with the following curt reply :

" Geheimrat von Holstein begs to be excused.
He does not possess court dress."

This invariable answer was addressed to four
Imperial Chancellors in turn, to Bismarck,
Caprivi, Hohenlohe and finally to Bülow. For
forty years the same preposterous excuse was
made to serve.

All other official invitations were similarly
refused, including Court commands, and so the
incredible state of affairs grew up—the powerful
director of the foreign policy of the German
Empire never crossed the threshold of the White
Hall.

On the 22nd of March, 1887, the aged
Emperor's birthday, Holstein received the

Order of the Crown. When Herbert Bismarck asked if he was pleased, "faithful Fritz" grunted :

"It is just about as ridiculous to have this cross as not to have it."

## 14

## FRAU VON LEBBIN'S SALON

GEHEIMRAT VON LEBBIN died in 1884 of cancer of the tongue. For some years his widow lived a retired and quiet life in her home Am Karlsbad, 27. Then she gradually began to renew old friendships and contrived to give an individuality to her salon that surprised even the most exacting.

Holstein was the widowed lady's general adviser, while she filled a gap in his bachelor existence. They became intimate friends and Cupid did not interfere to disturb their happiness. Holstein had never been capable of love, less than ever now that he was wedded to his work.

Every salon in the later Bismarck days was bound to take sides : with the Chancellor or against him. Until Lebbin's death his house had been definitely hostile ; his widow inaugurated a new era and encouraged as far as possible the Pro's and Anti's to meet at her house.

One day Holstein called at Frau Lebbin's and found a strange lady installed in the drawing-room, flashily got-up and somewhat over stout. The maid-servant had announced her as Frau von Wallhoffen. Now Holstein was music-deaf and never went near the Opera, so he had not the faintest suspicion that his *vis-à-vis* was the famous Pauline Lucca, the dramatic cantatrice. She, on the other hand, knew all about him, for she was a welcome visitor at Court and *au courant* of all the busy rumours that fluttered round the Empress concerning " His Excellency the Spectre."

On seeing a stranger, Holstein was inclined to beat a retreat, when he heard himself addressed :

" Do you know where I have just come from, Geheimrat ?  Straight from the Crown Prince's. Dear me!  I'm sorely afraid his Royal Highness won't hold out much longer.  I had a word with Bramann, he talks of an operation and wants the Prince to go immediately to San Remo.  The Empress had a tea-party yesterday and the Emperor had to send an apology because he wasn't well.  Schneider told me afterwards on the stairs that the poor old man is failing.  It's too sad, and Prince William is such a boy ! "

Here was news that might have value.  The nightmare that the telegram from Varzin had conjured up had faded harmlessly, but here was a new danger : a possible change of monarch.  He allowed the talkative Pauline—who for all her garrulity never ceased to be amusing—to entertain him ; asked questions, even paid her court, and so pre-occupied were the pair with each other that they did not mark the entry of other guests.

One sentence from the general conversation penetrated Holstein's abstraction :

"I don't consider success the touchstone of a character's historical importance, but justice and truth and humanity. Otherwise the most unprincipled blackguards would often appear the greatest figures in History."

"Meaning me?" wondered Holstein, distrustful as ever.

"Who is that?" he asked his new acquaintance.

"You mean the small man over there with the pince-nez and a ribbon behind his ear? He's a journalist, Wittkowski, but he calls himself Harden, too. He is a spiritual cave-dweller, I warn you, Baron."

Wittkowski, in his corner, was continuing:

"We disciples of Bismarck must not forget that the greatest creations must never be allowed to fossilise, but must perpetually adapt themselves to keep pace with moral, national and economic development."

"Quite true," said Holstein to himself, and turning again to Pauline Lucca:

"A Jew, of course?"

"Why, naturally! But now I must move off. I see Schleinitz over there."

Holstein started. "Gone. Why did she treat me so cavalierly? That sort of thing hurts."

He turned to go, and had already got into the corridor when his friend and hostess overtook him, took away his coat and led him into an anteroom.

" Tell me, Fritz. Do you know who will be the new Imperial Chancellor ? "

" Imperial Chancellor ? " he echoed in dazed tones.

" Now, Fritz, do be sensible. Schleinitz wants to talk to you about it. The Emperor has only a few weeks to live. The Crown Prince's life is despaired of and he's just gone off to the Riviera to die. The new Kaiser is bound to take a new line. . . ."

He was face to face with his enemy. Each stood alone.

By that evening the Bismarck fortress had lost its first defender. The Anti's had secured the allegiance of the indispensable Holstein against the moment when the change should come.

## 15

# THE PASSING OF THE OLD PRUSSIA

ALL the bells of Berlin are tolling. The boom of saluting cannon is heard from the Lustgarten. The dense crowds who have stationed themselves along the Charlottenburg Chausee are dressed in black to pay the last tribute to the old Emperor.*

A squadron of the Garde du Corps passes at the trot. The head of the mourning cortège is seen reaching the Brandenburg Gate. The music of the First Foot Guards is heard, the band of that regiment which the deceased monarch entered as a Lieutenant seventy years ago—in the days of the Wars of Liberation.

Holstein reflected over it all. He was not in his place in the ranks of the Foreign Office officials. He had lost himself in the ordinary crowd near the Schloss Bellevue.

" Ninety-one years old. Still his death has come too soon."

While the old Emperor was being laid to rest,

* William I., born 1797, King of Prussia 1861, Emperor of Germany 1871, died 1888.

his heir was under the surgeon's knife and doomed to die. While they were playing funeral marches here, the mourners were already speculating about the young Emperor, whom no one yet knew anything about.

The dead man's first adjutant, Count Perponcher, passed, bearing the cushion on which the orders rested. Then came the coffin on a gun-carriage. Holstein made obeisance. His homage was genuine, for, though he had not known the old Kaiser personally, he had sincerely reverenced him. William I., with his modesty and his Prussian integrity, was the living demonstration of the soundness of conservative thought, was the perfection of a Prussian king.

Young Prince William followed the coffin—alone. A whisper ran through the crowd.

" There he is."

Holstein gazed attentively. Ere long this boy would be his master. Bismarck came next, and Holstein, who had been craning forward, instinctively drew back into the crowd. To evade the ceremonial he had reported himself sick at the Office to-day. Next Bismarck walked the aged Field Marshal, Count Moltke, in his furs. The third of that great trio, Roon, had already joined a larger army.* Then the new generation followed endlessly.

Holstein gazed long and earnestly after the

* Field Marshal Count von Roon, Prussian Minister of War, died 1879.

66

cortège. Its destination was the mausoleum at Charlottenburg, where rested the Kaiser's father and mother and Queen Luise. This is the last ceremonial procession of its kind, the Old Prussia is passing with this old man's funeral.

As the Geheimrat went home along the Linden he saw lights burning in the "Kommode." The Empress Augusta had stayed at home and was now no doubt seated between the two Victorias, for the daughter-in-law had summoned her mother from England to stand by her in the hour of stress.

"Will they keep on the great Imperial Chancellor?"

Holstein was ready for all eventualities, whatever the royal ladies might decide.

## 16

## HOLSTEIN WINS EULENBURG

HOLSTEIN made it his business to get hold of one of the medical men who was attending the Crown Prince, one on whose discretion he could rely. He found what he wanted in the person of Dr. Bramann, an ambitious young doctor, the right hand of Professor Bergmann. The Geheimrat was not long in divining that the doctor was longing to be made Physician in Ordinary, and, if possible, to be ennobled. Holstein promised everything, though in fact he had no influence over the household appointments. He felt it important to keep himself fully informed. From Bramann's reports it was clear that the end was not far off. This information was in direct contradiction to the optimistic bulletins which were being published about the royal invalid's health, but it seemed beyond a doubt that the new Emperor had lost his speech.

Holstein heard from Potsdam that Prince William had sent the Chancellor some decrees which in his impatience he had already drafted so as to secure Bismarck's approval in advance. These essays had been firmly but courteously returned to their royal author with the suggestion that His Imperial Highness would be well advised to remember that Germany still possessed a modest constitution and a body of Federal Princes. Rumour ran that the Prince was wild at the rebuke.

Holstein asked himself : if so slight an incident could already cause a breeze, what would the tempest be like when things grew serious ?

If Bismarck was dismissed, his henchman Holstein would go too ; some hedging would be necessary. So he laid down a new line of action. He would not break with the Bismarcks, but he would quietly support the party of Schleinitz and Loë, for the new Chancellor would certainly come from that group. The most important thing was to acquire influence over the coming Kaiser, or at least find means of keeping himself informed of how things were going in that quarter. One man could serve his purpose : Philip Eulenburg. He was playing David to the young Prince's Jonathan.

So he wrote a letter to Eulenburg with whom he was essentially just as much out of tune as with Arnim. It was never difficult to get a hold on men of this type, who are sentimental, vain and superficial—or so he judged. You must appeal to their weaknesses.

Holstein made an appointment to meet Philip Eulenburg in the Hotel de Rome. He knew that Phili would dearly like to go as Ambassador to

Munich, so he dangled this bait in front of him. Eulenburg was, of course, rather young for Munich : some intermediate step would be inevitable. About Karlsruhe now ? Eulenburg held up his hands in horror. He shuddered at the thought of such a backwater. Stuttgart would be preferable. Holstein promised that he should have Stuttgart next year.

That little matter being settled, the Geheimrat now came forward with his counter-requests, enquiries and desires. He took care to take payment in advance for his promises. Philip Eulenburg told him everything he had heard in Potsdam. When Holstein pressed him to promise him unconditional loyalty and to use his whole influence with Prince William on his behalf, the Count retorted, laughing :

" I can't compete with Saint Kunigunde who used to hang her gloves on a sun's ray to dry. But I'll see what I can do."

" Odd to compare himself with a woman saint," reflected Holstein. He proved the other with his eyes while his thoughts reverted to a rainy night : " Krause ! " A second memory emerged : " Hoffmann. Who is Hoffmann ? "

" What are you staring at me like that for ? " enquired Phili, vaguely disquieted. And to turn the conversation to a lighter topic he started telling an anecdote :

" Can you imagine this ? I was at the Bismarcks' yesterday and the Chancellor showed me

70

a score of Beethoven's *Eroica* which Hans von Bülow had presented to him. I suggested he should send Bülow the Second Part of *Faust*\* in return. By the way, did you know that Bernhard Bülow is here? He blew in from Bucharest yesterday."

Holstein started as if a tarantula had stung him.

" Bülow here? I hadn't heard a word of it."

The ingenuous Eulenburg went on :

" I rather think Prince William sent for him. I expect he's got a summons to be at Potsdam to-morrow."

Holstein spent that evening hot on the trail of Bernhard Bülow. But Bülow seemed to have got wind of the pursuit, and was nowhere to be found.

\* See note, p. 101.

## 17

### A TRIP TO THE HARZ

EULENBURG and Bramann had now been secured (Bernhard Bülow had gone off to Flottbeck and was not expected back for four days). They had both promised to telegraph at once if anything special happened. So Holstein left his little flat in charge of the faithful housekeeper, Frau Röber, and betook himself in this July, 1888, for a holiday to his beloved Harz.

After his appointment to the Foreign Office he never travelled abroad. Why go to the Riviera, Egypt or Greece? The Harz was his substitute for them all. He pursued this course so consistently that another curious fact is to be chronicled : This man who for over thirty years directed German Foreign Policy made no attempt to visit, or revisit, or learn to know, any foreign country.

His letters of this period, and later, have been published (Richard Schröder Verlag, Berlin, W. 62). They are short reports, mostly addressed to Frau von Lebbin. It is remarkable how much attention he devotes to his physical ego. He talks of clothes and food in true bachelor fashion. He writes, for instance :

" Hahnenklee is a place where a clean shirt will last two days. . . .

" Supper was rather a failure. We were having scrambled eggs, and this dish is governed by exactly the opposite principle from Sodom and Gomorrah. In the latter case—if I remember right—ten just men would have sufficed to save the whole degenerate collection of " bad eggs " —but the ten just men were lacking. With scrambled eggs *one* bad one is enough to wreck the lot : and the one was not lacking ! . . .

" Alcohol is simply suicide for anyone with diabetes. . . .

" Any climbing I do has to be uphill ; I can't tackle a downhill climb because my pince-nez tend to fall off. . . .

" Talking of a forester who had been turned off, mine host told me that they had found all the raised platforms in the neighbourhood (they are put up for shooting big game, and are 15 to 20 feet above the ground) had been covertly sawn through, so that anyone using them would inevitably have broken an arm or a leg. Goethe's idea of peace among the tree tops * is false.

> The great storm is the foe
> Of wild life, high and low †

sings Walther von der Vogelweide. And Walther is right."

Many of his anecdotes show his humour and understanding of children.

* Über allen Gipfeln ist Ruh      † Das Wild und das Gewürme
  In allen Wipfeln spürest du        Die kämpfen grosse Stürme.
  Kaum einen Hauch.

" I have to wear my cataract glasses for reading. When I want to see properly in the ordinary way I have to close the right eye. Children often think I am winking at them and inviting them to play. Yesterday evening four little girls were at the railway station—between five and eight they were, I suppose. I looked at them and they ran up suddenly and said, laughing : ' Good evening, Uncle,' and made little curtsies and shook hands."

The voice of the Prussian Junker is heard:

" The youngster here has to walk three or four miles out and the same distance back. A younger brother looks a bit delicate. That is Nature's survival of the fittest. And really, when you see the miserable scurvy-ridden litters some families leave behind them, you can't help thinking it would be better for humanity if they could all be subjected to this same stern examination for existence."

The enemy of Social Democracy speaks in :

" The common people here in Rübeland look very different from ours. The men are defiant, the younger womenfolk shameless. So much for factory influence ! "

This volume also contains some verses—the only ones of Holstein's recorded :

> Now with nice rain I might oblige you,
> But ditto verses have I none.
> Not mine, my friend, to stand beside you,
> Poet and minister in one.

74

For Pegasus's wing and feather
    I have but walking-stick and shoes ;
I'd rather wait for sunny weather
    To come—if I'm allowed to choose.

He gives Frau von Lebbin a witty account of a little episode in Berlin :

" The concierge's daughter of our mansions has just been married to someone or other. I don't know either of the parties by sight, but I have often run across the kiddy. It isn't yet able to walk quite alone, so the marriage can't be called too belated."

These few samples of his published letters throw some light on Holstein's character. In spite of their humour they have a malevolent undertone that is highly characteristic.

On the 15th of June a telegram from Bramann reached him in Schierke :

" Come at once."

In his flat he found an express letter awaiting him. News from Phili ! He opened it in all haste. It contained an invitation to an Edith Walker concert at the Singakademie. The singer was to render Eulenburg's " Märchen von der Freiheit."

" And at such a moment ! " groaned Holstein. " Instead of news he sends me concert tickets. And you're expected to collaborate in high politics with a dreamer of that sort ! "

Then he set to work. There was no time to lose, to secure a place in the sun.

## 18

## THE RE-INSURANCE PACT

BISMARCK had concluded, on the 18th of June, 1887, the so-called Re-Insurance Pact with Russia. This was a secret agreement according to which each of the two signatory Powers was pledged to maintain a benevolent neutrality if the other was attacked without provocation. The treaty was valid for three years. It would therefore lapse in 1890. Bismarck was all for renewing it, Holstein was against. It is true that he later emphatically denied having been responsible for cancelling the Re-Insurance Pact with Russia, but there is no question that it was he who was behind this fateful step.

He was well aware that the young Kaiser looked askance at the treaty, and he made use of Bötticher, who had already deserted the Bismarcks, to torpedo its renewal. He had secured the co-operation of Captain von Kessel in Potsdam, who had been in the Emperor Frederick's service up to the last, and was looking about for new prospects. Kessel was an able man who later became Chief Officer Commanding in the Marks, and meantime he secured the ear of the new

Kaiser, the more readily that his opinions ran counter to Bismarck's. The new monarch was only too ready to forget the counsels of his dying grandfather, William I. : " Stand by the Tsar, my boy. Don't abandon the alliance with Russia ! "

The Chancellor was soon informed of these designs. He also learned all about the deserters from his camp. The wrath of Herbert Bismarck and of his greater father was working up for an explosion.

The decision to force Bismarck's resignation had been taken in January, 1890. The young Kaiser was only waiting for a suitable opportunity and a convenient excuse.

As Secretary of State, Herbert Bismarck employed every expedient, and even lectured the Emperor in his father's name in the endeavour to save the Re-Insurance Pact. He found it difficult to preserve his calm, for this treaty, which was the fruit of his father's unremitting labour, was now to be swept away by irresponsible amateurs. Herbert Bismarck clearly saw how incalculable the consequences were which would follow on the exposure of the Eastern Front. He made the greatest efforts to avert the disaster, less for love of his new sovereign than of his father's life work.

He betook himself to the Chief of the Central Office, the Registrar Mechler, and demanded the original documents of the Re-Insurance Pact.

" They are with Geheimrat von Holstein," was the reply.

He went to look up Holstein, but was refused admittance :

" The Herr Geheimrat has a visitor with him."

He was too proud to ask who the visitor might be, so he posted himself at the window of the adjacent waiting-room to see for himself. Half an hour later the visitor went out : it was General Count Waldersee.

Very little is known about that last conversation which led to the final breach between Holstein and the Bismarcks. It is clear that it must have been a heated one, since even the padded doors could not keep secret the fact that there had been a quarrel.

Herbert : " So you have been discussing the cancellation of the Pact with the future Imperial Chancellor, Herr Geheimrat ! But the end is not yet. Wait and see ! " And bitterly he added : " The rat deserts the sinking ship."

Holstein burst out—little left of " Faithful Fritz " !—" I protest against the imputation. You gain nothing by reminding me how you have treated me like a galley slave or beast of burden, whom you could exploit for your dreams of power. You know how deeply I have honoured the Chancellor, your father, and you have traded on my loyalty and affection to squeeze me like an orange and discard the rind. You made me your tool to wreck Arnim, you made me an outcast. All that is your doing, Herbert!"

"You will probably now be Secretary of State," retorted Herbert, "and my successor, and so you will achieve your ambition. That will comfort you for the fact that you owe all your success to my father. Without him you would not be what you are, Holstein. But there is no use in prolonging the conversation. I should be obliged for the papers!"

Holstein surrendered them. He was trembling so much that his eyeglasses fell off. Without a backward glance Herbert Bismarck left the room.

The Geheimrat reeled like a drunken man as he groped his way home. He was practically blind without his glasses. He fetched another pair from home and then enquired at the Palace who would be Adjutant on duty to-morrow: Captain von Kessel.

That very day two letters were despatched, to Waldersee and to Kessel respectively! At all costs the audience of Herbert Bismarck, Secretary of State, with his Imperial Majesty must be prevented.

## 19

## A STROLL WITH "LA CONTESSINA"

FRAU VON LEBBIN'S tea-party was over. Holstein took leave of Pauline Lucca :

" It is always a privilege to meet the Prima Donna of our Opera ! "

" The attributes of a Prima Donna, my dear Baron, are usually supposed to be vanity, caprice, jealousy and spite. The flattering description would seem more applicable to your circle than to mine," was the singer's significant reply.

Frau von Bülow's husband had been detained ; the hostess requested Holstein to escort the lady home. Holstein offered his arm to the quondam Countess Dönhoff. She had recently been divorced and was now married to Bernhard Bülow. At court they had nicknamed her " La Contessina." As the daughter of the famous Donna Laura and step-daughter of the great Italian statesman Marco Minghetti, she had always enjoyed the reputation of being an able woman. It was late. Holstein took the path through the Tiergarten, which was then much more densely planted than nowadays in its more English style. The Geheimrat took advantage of this opportunity to retail to the Contessina the most alarming stories. It was growing darker and darker. She urged him to press on. She was much relieved when at last they came safely to the Brandenburg Gate and she finally reached the great hall of the hotel, where she found her husband waiting. He and Holstein were old acquaintances, and the warmth of the Geheimrat's greeting was not lessened by the suspicion that Bülow was a coming man.

But when Bülow began to speak, Holstein's presence of mind almost forsook him for a moment. "The voice? The voice! This is the voice heard that night in "The Fleet." This is Hoffmann."

Frau von Bülow had gone straight up to her room. The strain and excitement of the walk had brought on a fit of hysterical crying. When her husband solicitously asked what the matter was, she confessed amidst her tears :

"You can't think how uncanny it was walking through the jungly darkness of the Park alone with that man. It is the first time in my life I have been terrified like this. Do you know, his eyes reminded me of that weird Dr. Mirakel."

"Yes, I remember. . . . Beetz sang the part," Bülow pursued. "It was in *Hoffmann's Tales*. Théâtre paré."

Holstein, of course, knew nothing of the Contessina's tears. But by a strange coincidence he was also thinking of a " Hoffmann "; not of the poet, Ernst Theodor Amadeus Hoffmann, author of the *Tales*, but of that midnight Hoffmann of " The Fleet." His Hoffmann was a diplomat.

How did this man come to be in that disreputable den ? He pursued his reflections : " Bülow *must* be in love with his wife. He laboured most perseveringly to secure her divorce from Dönhoff. He brought influence to bear on the Vatican till the Holy Father was persuaded to annul the previous marriage : all in order to win this woman and then ; he goes to ' The Fleet ' ? " Holstein came to a full stop : " What a fool I am making of myself ! Bülow got there just as I did, by accident. It was pouring and he took shelter. . . . Yet he seemed known in the place . . . they called him ' Hoffmann ' and the other ' Krause.' And what was Eulenburg-Krause doing in that low pub at night in company with painted-up bogus sailormen ? Isn't he a married man, happy, the father of several children ? How can it all be pieced together ? "

Then the Geheimrat remembered a book which said that men with this peculiar disposition were often able men, had effeminate ways and gestures, and were fond of scent. It all tallied. They *were* both clever men, Philip Eulenburg had even a touch of genius, and they both perfumed themselves. Holstein had often noticed it with distaste.

He could not bear to smell scent off a man. But these things were hardly proof!

Hatzfeld had once called Bernhard von Bülow an actor. Was this marriage of his just " theatre," a means to an end? Was the Italian woman a blind to help him to climb the Capitoline Rock to gain entrance to the Palazzo Caffarelli,* as a stepping stone to higher heights?

" If so, why this criminal carelessness? C'est plus qu'un crime, c'est une faute! "

Having reached this point in his meditations, Holstein turned into the Französische Strasse to think the matter out, over a glass of Borchardt's old Bordeaux.

* The German Embassy in Rome.

## 20

## MR. PARISER

WHEN a young Guardsman in the 90's found himself in straits for money he would go to Pariser. This so-called "Banker" lived in a back house behind the Karlstrasse guarded by an immense bull-dog, to protect him at night from uninvited guests. His clients often came at midnight while play in the clubs was still running high. No one remembered Pariser's ever being seen in the street. Any sum you liked to name was always lying ready in his drawer. He had a carefully compiled card-index which enabled him to judge just how far he could safely go with any given customer. The interest was strictly "legal." He only asked a little commission of 10 per cent., and to simplify the transaction he deducted this, with the interest, in advance. The little bill was a pure formality. The loan must be repaid punctually, otherwise the enquiry machine was set in motion and that was apt to end in information being lodged with the young man's commanding officer.

Holstein was just busy composing his instructions—celebrated and dreaded—for representatives abroad, when Mr. Pariser was announced.

Never having heard the name, the Geheimrat let the visitor wait a bit, and since the name suggested a Jew, there was all the less need for haste. Holstein did not love Jews. He would make use of them of course on occasion, but only when compelled, and never willingly. He signed the instructions to the diplomats, but not all of them. It was one of his peculiarities that he never put his name to a document which might prove in any way compromising. There is scarcely a telegram extant with his signature. His communications were ruthlessly outspoken; he stopped at nothing, shrank from no tactlessness, no threat. The recipients of his letters might well take fright when the Geheimrat in Berlin threw their debts or their *aventures amoureuses* in their teeth, rebuked them for getting advances from the office or commented in other ways on their private affairs. They were for ever being surprised afresh. "How *does* he get to know and put all these things together?"

It sometimes happened that he would himself lend money to a friend: if he needed him and thought his position insecure. For the most part, however, his attitude was destructive. A young Embassy Secretary, writing to his sister, hit the nail on the head: "Holstein presides over our lives like a basilisk."

One more telegram to Hatzfeld in London. The text was short and unambiguous: "Demand Chirol's immediate recall, otherwise he will be

deported." This Chirol was *The Times* corre-
spondent and had been for years a friend of
Holstein's. Now some baseless suspicion had
poisoned the friendship and hostility ensued.

Holstein treated all his friends in the same way
—converted them into his best enemies. In his
old age he reflected with cynical resignation : " I
have called a very few men by their Christian
names—and there are no people I am now on
worse terms with ! "

Chirol shared with another colleague, Mr
Saunders, the privilege of being, first a friend,
then an enemy of Holstein's. Holstein had been
on a most cordial footing with Frau Haynauer
and Saunders, her English son-in-law, until one
day the Geheimrat thought he got a whiff of
treachery and a complete breach followed. In
this case, too, Holstein insisted that Saunders
should leave Germany. He worked up a sort of
persecution-neurosis in connection with both
these newspaper correspondents, though in fact
the behaviour of both was scrupulously correct.

At last Pariser was admitted. Flinching before
the glance of the dreaded autocrat, the usurer
stammeringly began. He spoke of the price of
money, and how no one on 'change exactly knew
what was going to happen next ; relations with
Russia seemed so hazy. If it were certain whether
the Re-Insurance Pact was to be cancelled or
not . . .

Holstein let him flounder to the end. Now and then he slowly winked one eye, a gesture which Pariser, like the children in the Harz, misinterpreted. He felt his meaning understood and finally blurted out the real object of his mission : he would like to do a deal with Holstein on the strength of the latter's inner knowledge of the political situation.

" Well, well, and what would be my share ? "

" We should halve the profits," replied the delighted Israelite.

" One of your predecessors in the Foreign Office here—he's dead now—gave me a useful little bit of information once and we each pocketed a monkey."

Pariser rubbed his hands at the recollection.

Holstein rose to his feet. His fingers had ceased their well-known drumming on the table, and with an icy voice he cut in—" You've come to the wrong address, my good sir. I shall have you arrested for the attempted bribery of His Imperial Majesty's State officials ! Eh ? "

Pariser fell from the clouds. He had had a totally different conception of " His Excellency the Spectre." He started incoherent prayers for mercy, got all sorts of titles mixed up in his anxiety, and finally burst into tears. After a pause :

" I've thought it over, Mr. Pariser," said Holstein mercilessly. " How much did you say you had earned ?—I don't ask the dead man's name—£500, I think. You will write me a cheque here and now for this sum. And as you happen to be on the spot I should like a look at your note book. You have various diplomats amongst the clients on your register if I am not mistaken. . . . But perhaps my demands seem rather high? There is a police post over there in the Imperial Chancellery. I press this button and . . ."

The wretched victim writhed and wailed; it would be ruin for him. . . . Holstein interrupted brusquely:

"It's not a question of your ruin but of the ruin of others through you. Yes or no? Choose. I do not change my mind."

The banker tried to rescue at least his list of clients, speaking of "honour" and "discretion," to which the Geheimrat scathingly retorted:

"'Honour,' Mr. Pariser, is a word whose meaning you are incapable of grasping! My time is of some value."

With a despairing nod the moneylender indicated his acceptance of the conditions and silently pushed his note book across the table. Holstein turned over the pages. Meantime he had rung for a messenger:

"Take Mr. Pariser to the Head Office of the Treasury. He has been so kind as to offer a donation of £500 to the Military Orphans' Fund. He will write a cheque and when Herr Hofrat Müller has cashed it at the bank he will give Mr. Pariser a receipt."

Holstein failed to see the hand which Pariser held out. When the door had closed behind the visitor the Geheimrat's eye still rested reflectively on the empty chair before him :

" Niemals, jamais, never ! " he muttered.

## 21

# BISMARCK'S FAREWELL TO THE FOREIGN OFFICE

MARCH, 1890. The Kaiser had summoned all his commanding Generals to Berlin. Calmly and practically he laid the situation before them. He proved to them that a fresh method of handling the labour question was necessary to allay agitation and to check the growth of Social Democracy.

"The Imperial Chancellor is unflinchingly opposed to any compromise in these matters. He is determined to maintain through thick and thin an out-of-date Cabinet order of September 8th, 1852, on which the authority of the Minister-President is based."

The Kaiser added that he did not attach so much importance to the revocation of the order itself, but he did very much deprecate its being made the pretext for keeping him, the Emperor, aloof from all State business.

Whereupon he laid document after document on the table, pointing out that every one of these papers had been dealt with by the Chancellor alone without his having been consulted. These papers included extremely important news from

Russia, a weighty report from Odessa which bore directly on the Russian Pact, a question which was at the moment in the foreground and of decisive importance.

Further, the Kaiser was constrained to confess that the Chancellor had openly expressed to the French Ambassador in Berlin his anger against his Imperial master and his dissatisfaction with things in general.

The generals were deeply impressed. It was perfectly clear that two governments could not exist side by side, and they heartily sympathised with the young War Lord who was seeking their moral support for a breach with Bismarck.

The Chancellor's resignation was accepted.

The Kaiser was genuinely anxious to mitigate the pain involved and to retain Herbert Bismarck as Secretary of State for Foreign Affairs. But the Bismarcks were irreconcilable. They would have neither part nor lot in the new era. They packed up.

Holstein wandered through the streets like Ahasuerus. He tried to ascertain what was going on in the Palace. But no one could tell him. Generals are not loquacious. If his favourite, Waldersee, becomes Chancellor, Holstein will reign in foreign affairs, for Waldersee intends to dispense with a Secretary of State, at any rate for the present.

It was like a conclave. The populace crowded before the Palace gates to hear the result of this royal council. Smoke could be seen from the chimneys, but it gave no clue to the draught that was being brewed. At last one name was heard : " Caprivi ! "

Who on earth might he be ? Holstein dashed into the Hotel de Rome, took down Army Lists and Gotha Almanacks : a general from Hanover. He made enquiries : " A decent fellow, true as steel, but the pure soldier. Not a shadow of diplomacy about him."

" Better even than Waldersee," he chuckled.

Meanwhile, the Foreign Office was abuzz with preparation. All the Councillors, Chancellery Officials and staff ranged themselves in the long corridor—each at the door of his own office, to form the last guard of honour for their honoured Chief. Accompanied by his son Herbert, Otto von Bismarck left his room at the Foreign Office for the last time. His face showed sorrow and controlled emotion. It looked as if he would fain have spoken, then he sighed and silently shook hands with each in turn. None of his officials ever forgot the impressiveness of this leave-taking. The giant figure paced slowly down through the ranks of his colleagues, past the conspicuously empty doorway of Geheimrat von Holstein, down the flight of entrance steps, where the well-timed carriage silently drove up.

The whole episode lasted only a few minutes and evoked an eerie feeling of foreboding.

When they were seated in the carriage, Herbert remarked:

"They were all there: only the Demon was missing," to which the father replied, slowly and with emphasis:

"If a demon is a spirit which is afraid to face the light, then Holstein is in truth the Demon."

Then his features grew set. Old Frau von Hülsen, who saw him at Lehrte junction, wrote in her diary:

"I saw to-day the incarnate soul of Germany, and mourn to-day for a Germany who has lost her soul."

II. CAPRIVI [1890—1894]

## 22

## CHANGES

THE first thing Holstein accomplished in the chaos of those early days after Bismarck's departure was to get Count Berchem out of the Foreign Office and instal in his stead the new Secretary of State, Baron Marschall,* the Kaiser's choice.

Amongst various despatches from foreign representatives Holstein had noticed in particular those of a certain Major von Engelbrecht. He gave admirable hints for dealing with Italy, more particularly tips about King Humbert and his minister the Marchese de Rudini. The fellow was growing too important. When Holstein heard that Engelbrecht had sent reports from the King of Italy direct to the Emperor, instead of through the Foreign Office, he got his teeth in.

He laid the matter before Caprivi: " The Ambassadors are groping in the dark if their military attachés pursue a policy of their own behind their Chief's back. The military must forthwith be fully subordinated to the Emperor's accredited representative."

Caprivi, during his whole term of office as

* Marschall von Bieberstein.

Chancellor, was never able to shake off the feeling that, as he put it :

" This Holstein is a perfect hedgehog. You can roll him over any way you like—but you never see his face."

He gave in, seeing no alternative. Egged on by Holstein, he even persuaded the Kaiser himself to rob his military attachés of their independence. When Waldersee called the Emperor's attention to the fact that in Bismarck's time it was always the military despatches which proved to be right and that the late Chancellor had always attached primary importance to them, he got the gruff reply :

" Well, that's just another reason for doing the opposite."

One evening Caprivi dropped into Holstein's room, where the light was always burning later than in anyone else's, and complained :

" France and Russia are getting more and more shameless."

The Geheimrat raised his eyes with a groan and said :

" These unfortunate relations with France and Russia are the legacy which Bismarck has left the Foreign Office ! "

Holstein's next aim was to get rid of Waldersee. He was the only person who knew the ins and outs of the double game the Geheimrat had been playing during Bismarck's last months. There was no longer the fear of his becoming Chancellor, but he must be got out of the position of Chief of the General Staff, for Holstein is suspicious and doesn't want him there.

In this year, 1891, while Eulenburg was absent as Ambassador in Stuttgart, a certain von Helldorff had the Emperor's ear. Holstein supplied him with material for an intrigue against Waldersee which progressed so successfully that the Kaiser finally made Count Schlieffen Chief of the General Staff and gave Waldersee a Corps. Holstein, through Helldorff, proposed the XIII. Corps. Its station was Stuttgart. Now a Prussian was none too welcome in Württemberg at the best of times. The Emperor was inclined to think this post rather a come-down for his General, when the Helldorff-Holstein pair hit on a diabolical idea:

Let Waldersee hold a great Army Inspection in Stuttgart for all the south German States to attend. This would put Waldersee in a position of authority over them all, including even Prinz Luitpold, who was his senior in military service: there would be a glorious flare-up.

If this was not enough, Phili could be enlisted to devise and carry out any further plans on the spot. Waldersee refused to walk into the snare and tendered his resignation.

This was more than Holstein had ventured to hope for, but he threw his cap into the air too

99

soon. The Kaiser had no mind to see his deserving General unemployed. He assigned the IX. (Altona) Corps to Waldersee, hoping thereby to build a bridge to Friedrichsruh * across which he might ultimately reach a reconciliation with the ex-Chancellor. Holstein was panicstricken. This was unforeseen. Reconciliation! Return! The game would be up!

Misfortunes seldom come singly : the Court Marshal, von Liebenau, was dismissed, and in his stead there entered on the stage the finest figure of William the Second's *régime*, the incorruptible Count August Eulenburg! The Geheimrat's evil magic would recoil powerless here.

Holstein had never been a soldier, never even a Corps student, though he had been at the University at Bonn. He had, however, an old pensioner of his there, a retired magistrate whom he had known in his undergraduate days, from whom he continued to get reports of everything that happened.

Since most of the Borussia † students used to go into the Diplomatic, he could find out, even before they entered the service, all about their gifts and temperaments, and in particular their attitude to the three great sciences : Women,

* The home of Bismarck's old age in the Saxon Forest near Hamburg. Purchased with a grant made to him in 1871 after the creation of the German Empire.

† Borussia, Latin for Prussia. The name of a famous student corps in Bonn.

Beer and Cards. This agent of Holstein's reported in May, 1891, to Berlin :

" His Majesty was here, attended a Kneipe and walked all round the town last night, dressed up in the coloured coat of a corps student accompanying Count Rex to the station. All classes of the population feel indignant."

" One day masquerading in a beerjacket, the next in ermine ! " murmured Holstein to himself. He cautiously burned the message in the flame of his candle, then took up his pen and wrote to Philip Eulenburg—of whose loyalty he felt assured—these prophetic words :

" I have just been rereading the Second Part of *Faust* and I am much struck by the resemblance between that Emperor * and ours. Ours also treats the task of governing as a kind of sport. Will he die in the purple, I wonder ? He isn't the right man, nor is this the right time to play with the people as with a toy. I am inclined to believe in a Republic—of which Bismarck laid the foundation—rather than in the entire collapse of the Empire."

* Goethe's prose sketch of *Faust Part II*. cast the Court scenes at Augsburg under the Emperor Maximilian (1493–1519), but the poet later shook off the fetters of actual history and depicted an abstract mediæval Emperor, " a prince," as he said to Eckermann, " possessed of every possible gift for losing his throne, which in fact he is ultimately successful in doing." (Oct. 1, 1827.)

## 23

# HOLSTEIN FADES OUT

ONE morning Holstein arrived in the office to find everything topsy-turvy with excitement. An army of charwomen were slithering on their knees over the floor, and even his own sacred den was flooded in the great clean-up campaign. Messengers, hung round with medals and decorations, were dashing about in their sprucest uniforms, the councillors were clad in black :

" His Majesty is coming ! He is going to have a look round himself ! "

An hour before the Emperor was due, the Geheimrat went out into the garden, sent for his hat and coat, and disappeared—as if the earth had swallowed him up. He was next heard of in the Pariser Platz on his way to Borchardt's. This art of sudden disappearance was one of his specialities; all his contemporaries record their admiration of the perfection to which he carried it.

At Borchardt's he summoned the boots :

" See here, my boy. If you would like to see the Kaiser, just run round to Kranzler's. He'll be passing by there in a moment. Here's a

trifle for you. As soon as he has gone, come
along back and tell me all about it."

As soon as he was sure that the Emperor was
safely back in his Palace, Holstein returned to his
desk.

The Empress had a tea-party that afternoon.
The Kaiser dropped in for a moment. He was
telling them all about Marschall and "the
Office." One of the Ladies-in-Waiting asked:

" And your Majesty saw Baron von Holstein?"

The Emperor replied, laughing:

" No. Holstein slipped through my fingers
this time. I must get hold of him one of these
days."

The Empress looked up in surprise at the name,
which had a ring of home about it * :

" Holstein? Who is he?"

And the Lord High Steward, Count Mirbach,
supplied the information :

" He is Marschall's right hand, and they've
nicknamed him ' His Excellency the Spectre.'
He's no great use for God, I hear."

* William II. had married in 1881 Auguste Viktoria of Schleswig-
Holstein (see note p. 205).

## 24

## PROPHETS AND FAITH-HEALERS

JUST at this time there was a craze for the occult. Even Waldersee and his wife belonged to a sect which was addicted to faith-healing, while prophesying was everywhere the rage. People had visions, and would go to obscure houses in the Krausenstrasse or the Gitschinerstrasse to hear elderly women broodingly mutter mysterious words. Each visitor swore by his own particular Cassandra. Waldersee's exercised no small influence on his fate. He jotted down one of her prophecies in his Diary under the date April 26, 1892—the truth of which time was to show:

" It must surely be clear to those who lead us that our position would be anything but favourable in the event of a war. We are confronted on both sides by a numerically superior enemy. An unsuccessful war would spell ruin. Other states can afford to be defeated. We cannot ! The German Empire will fall asunder, Prussia be beaten to her knees and reduced to less than the possessions she held before 1815, republican tendencies will assert themselves, the House of

Hohenzollern will go into exile, a life-and-death struggle awaits the Evangelical Church, poverty will be universal. This is no exaggeration. Such will be the inevitable consequence of a disastrous war which our present foreign policy is making all too possible."

If only Frau Grall of the Krausenstrasse could know how her prophecy had been fulfilled!

Philip Eulenburg, away in Munich, was keenly interested in all these mysterious forces. He took up spiritualism. He persuaded the Kaiser to accompany him to spiritualistic séances. When Holstein got wind of it he wrote savage letters to Phili. The latter was much surprised and answered innocently:

" I can assure you of one thing, Fritz: Providence has a great destiny in store for His Majesty."

## 25

## TWO DUELS

THE year 1892 saw the beginning of a particularly savage Press campaign against Count Waldersee. The whole history of this unfortunate man, from the moment that he took over the IX. Corps to the moment of his recall, is nothing but one long chain of defence, attack, repudiation of slander, fresh slander, justification and explanation.

Bismarck's proximity made the Count's position extremely difficult, for he now became in fact the intermediary between the Emperor and the ex-Chancellor.

Holstein watched these rapprochements with growing anxiety. He set the Press in motion and particularly the papers *Berliner Tageblatt*, *National-Zeitung*, *Reichsbote*, *Temps*, *Figaro*, *Pester Lloyd*.

When Waldersee learnt on good authority that Levysohn, the editor of the *Berliner Tageblatt*, was in the habit of visiting Holstein at home in the evening, and that he used to sneak in unobserved from the Königgrätzerstrasse, he had little doubt that the malicious attacks in which the *Tageblatt* was particularly distinguishing itself were prompted by the Geheimrat. He wrote a vigorous letter to Holstein, who replied by challenging him to fight. When the news reached Bismarck in Friedrichsruh the old warrior was delighted :

" Shoot straight, Waldersee ! The rascal deserves a bullet through his hide."

The Emperor, however, got wind of the projected duel and forbade it :

" Leave my Holstein in peace, can't you ? I'd never get another worker like him. It would be the last straw if he were to be shot down. He's a downright good fellow, Holstein."

This little episode was hardly over when a new campaign began in the *Zukunft* with an article called " Coming Men." A triumvirate of commanding generals was there spoken of, to Holstein's unfeigned delight. He was just going to call on Harden, hoping to complete his conversion to his own way of thinking in the matter, when another Harden article, " Camarilla," appeared in the *Leipziger Neueste Nachrichten*. This was the first use of that significant word that was later to become so familiar. Holstein was forced to recognise that while Harden was ready enough to criticise the military party, he was going to go further in the Holstein-Eulenburg-Kiderlen case. This was terrible : Holstein was on the scene too late.

Simultaneously, *Kladderadatsch* brought out a whole series about the " Oyster-Eater," the

" Sparrow " and the " Troubadour," which nicknames were transparently intended for Holstein, Kiderlen * and Eulenburg. Holstein scented Count Henckel, the reputed owner of the paper, behind these attacks. He sent him a challenge. Henckel named Waldersee as his second.

Countess Henckel and Frau von Lebbin already had visions of a green meadow in the morning mist, carriages, the doctor with bandages and two half-naked men bent on shooting each other dead.

The Kaiser went to Abbazia on the 30th May. He had heard about the *Kladderadatsch* article and excused Kiderlen from accompanying him because the article was also aimed at him. Meantime Holstein had engaged General von Bissing as his second against Henckel. Herbert Bismarck was in Berlin at the time and wrote home :

" I should just love to see Holstein at the moment silently stealing, with dagger drawn as it were, over the thick carpets of the palace."

Philip Eulenburg, who was in Abbazia with the Kaiser, contrived skilfully to wrest the dagger from his friend. His Majesty telegraphed to forbid the duel, and on this occasion referred to Holstein as " our pearl among officials."

* A jest may be intended about the " little sparrow " pastries [Spätzele] which are popular in Swabia and South Germany. Kiderlen-Wächter was a Swabian.

## 26

## HOLSTEIN'S NET

IT was Holstein's ambition to cover the whole of diplomatic Europe (and as further afield as possible) with a network of his spies who would keep him informed of everything, and who would at the same time be trustworthy and wholly devoted to himself. One of these was Solms, in whom he placed complete reliance; Paul Hatzfeld, in London, was another; Radolinski (or Radolin, as he now preferred to be called), whom he had known since the Bonn days, was a third. This Radolin is unique—the only man in Holstein's life who, without one single quarrel, remained his friend to the last. He wanted to enlist other stalwarts of the same kind, primarily Eulenburg, whom he hoped to get transferred to Vienna. The previous Viennese Ambassador, Reuss, had never been a friend of Holstein's, and Wedel, who was being talked of for the post, was probably a Bismarck man. Wedel must first be disposed of. That was a simple matter. The Geheimrat prompted the Austria-Hungarian Ambassador, Count Szögyenyi Marich, to call on Caprivi and drop the hint,

apparently as his own spontaneous comment, that
Wedel would not be so welcome in Vienna as
Count Eulenburg.

This didn't happen to be the fact, but the Chancellor would be glad to hear it, for it would be
welcome news to the Kaiser, who always thought
the genius of his beloved Phili was not sufficiently
known or appreciated.

Holstein was so anxious to pull this off that he
mystified the Austrian Ambassador by the lavish-
ness of his promises. Why should so trifling a
personal matter command so high a price?
Meantime, Bernhard von Bülow was sent to Rome
and the Emperor was fully in favour of the
appointment, and thought the selection a particularly happy one, since the Contessina was
always *persona grata* there. Roman Catholic circles
raised the objection that the Contessina's divorce
would exclude the pair from the more devout
Roman houses. To which Holstein curtly retorted that " people who feel like that have our
Embassy to the Vatican to amuse themselves
with." Holstein always looked on Roman
Catholics with suspicion.

Holstein recognised with pleasure, but—being
what he was—also with misgiving, that friend
Bernhard was the very man for Rome, for his
despatches had all those qualities the post
demanded. He anticipated that Bülow would
prove to be the future Secretary of State, the
successor to Marschall, under whom he, the

Geheimrat, would therefore some day be working. It was important to get a cinch on Bülow.

At this point Phili could be useful. His Vienna despatches were not a whit behind Bülow's in quality. Grip of a situation, power of expression, judgment, good counsel, a touch of genius, all blended in a brilliant style. But Phili was spending far too little time in the Metternichgasse,* far less than became the responsibilities of his post. Holstein was too shrewd to attack him directly, but he instigated a certain Count Stirum to prepare to ask this question in the Reichstag :

" Is it worth while for the Empire to support an expensive Embassy in Vienna if the Ambassador spends most of his time travelling about and seems the victim of a positive amusement-mania ? " The phrase " amusement-mania " was Holstein's.

The Emperor was furious, because it was he who perpetually sent for Phili to come from Vienna and join him ; and Holstein was glad that the Emperor should be annoyed, not least because in this way Count Stirum, whom Holstein disliked, would get into bad odour. The Geheimrat was always delighted to kill several birds with one stone.

Philip Eulenburg heard of the proposed Reichstag attack and begged Holstein to forestall it if he could. Nothing could of course be easier !

During these and the next few years Holstein

* The German Embassy in Vienna.

acted as a kind of mentor to Philip Eulenburg and
Bernhard Bülow, watching over them anxiously,
and even posing as mediator between them when
little jealousies cropped up. Phili was an open-
hearted fellow and often gave Holstein a glimpse
into his relations with Bülow. He showed him a
letter from "dear Bernhard" in which their
friendship was said to "have a touch of the
antique about it." He used to show him letters
full of quotations : "Why seek diligently after
the source of evil when the source of evil lies in
the very fact of existence ?" occurred in an
answer of his to Bülow. And when he woke on
the day of the first performance of his opera he
quoted—"I awoke one morning and found
myself famous ! "

Holstein, who was very widely read, made a
mental note :

"The first comes from Platen, the second from
Byron ! Ha, ha ! "

And his thoughts flew again to "Krause." A
letter of Bülow's to Phili, dated October 13th,
1893, had grave implications for "Hoffmann" :
"You are the Germanic-Hellenic type, I rather
the Prussian-Roman ; You are rather more the
cavalier, and I the soldier."

Holstein's conviction grew : "I've got them."

He read the words carefully through again. He
had to remember them till evening, till he should
have time to write them down at home.

While Phili was carefully replacing his letters

in his breast pocket a noise was heard next door (they were at Borchardt's). They enquired who was there. It was Herbert Bismarck with a lot of men friends. Herbert's voice was always loud. He could be heard through the wall shouting :

" Champagne. Hi! Bring Champagne ! "

Then he sang his favourite song of Duke Krock of Swabia, who rode out from Böblingen to lay-ay-ay wa-a-ste everything in the land of the Gaul !

Phili was sensitive to sound : he turned with impotent disgust to his senior. Holstein pondered awhile, like a doctor faced by a difficult diagnosis, then he said gravely :

" I am told he gargles with rum the first thing in the morning."

## 27

## AN OLD DRAWER

BY 1894 Holstein was almost blind. He could only see at all and recognise people with his glasses on. So his friend, Frau von Lebbin, " Lena " as his intimate circle called her, was obliged to come oftener to the Grossbeerenstrasse to keep an eye on things and see that the lonely man's house was properly run. Old " Röberchen," Holstein's faithful housekeeper, was not as young as she had been, and was afflicted with chronic forgetfulness.

In her tidyings up one day Lena found an old drawer with pictures of Schwedt, where Holstein was born, a photograph of himself and his contemporaries in their last year at school, souvenirs of his college life at Bonn and Berlin, of his early days as a barrister, of the various towns where he had been posted as a young diplomat : Rio de Janeiro, London, Washington, Stuttgart, Florence and Copenhagen. An old inkstand and penholder, carefully wrapped in paper, caught her attention :

" What on earth is this, Fritz ? " she asked.

Holstein had not touched the parcel for years ; he felt it :

" Ah, yes . . . that used to belong to Bismarck. Do you know, Lena, that inkstand and that penholder ought really to be in a museum. That is the very inkstand that was standing on his desk in Frankfurt on the 26th of February, 1871, when as Chancellor he signed the peace. I was his secretary in those days. He gave them to me as a souvenir. *Non ragioniam di lor!*" * And with this word of Dante's Vergil he passed on to other things.

Lena, however, stowed the precious writing-things carefully away, marvelling the while at all this man had lived through and the composure with which he talked of the great events in which he had borne a part.

Another drawer was full of studs, shoe-laces, the Hohenzollern domestic order and other decorations which he never wore and which were only in the way. Letters were scattered through the various drawers, all sorts of notes to him, some of them anonymous, some spiteful and abusive. One was scribbled on a piece of hand-made paper :

" Lucky dog ! Who like a hog, his belly doth fill with all he cannot swill."

The only thing she did not find was the little parcel, tied up with red ribbon, containing letters and a lock of hair, that was in those days almost obligatory.

Lena had access to everything and was allowed

* Speak not of them, but look and pass them by—Dante (Cary).

to read every line. Only the safe was sacred. It stood, sinister and silent, in the corner behind its locks. Fritz never opened it unless he was alone, and he always carried the key of it on his person.

When he died, this treasure-house was immediately and secretly bought in " by an interested party."

## 28

# NIGHT IN THE FOREST OF LIEBENBERG

THE *Kölnische Zeitung* of the 6th of October, 1894, published an article expressing gratification at the fact that the Kaiser was giving his support to the so-called " Revolutionary Bill " (Umsturzvorlage). The paper went on to express its pleasure that this meant a slap in the face for Philip Eulenburg, who was known to be against the Bill.

Holstein read the article in Berlin and sent it to Phili at Liebenberg,* where he was again staying. Phili telegraphed inviting Holstein to come at once, as he had some most important matters to discuss.

Great preparations had been going on in the Castle to provide a worthy reception for the all-powerful guest who was paying his first visit to Liebenberg. At the station Holstein announced that he regretted he could not come to the house. He must have his time with Phili alone and undisturbed. His host protested that his library had padded walls and they could be entirely private

---

* Philip zu Eulenburg's beloved country seat, where he wrote poetry, composed music and frequently entertained the Kaiser.

there. The Geheimrat would not hear of going to the house and proposed that their interview should take place in some little shooting box or other. Holstein's dread of society was unconquerable.

Philip Eulenburg has himself given a description of this interview in the moonlight under a pine in the Forest of Liebenberg. It can scarcely have been less dramatic than the evening walk through the Tiergarten with the Contessina. They first discussed foreign affairs and Holstein's desire to bring about an alliance between Germany, France and Russia. Phili was shocked at Holstein's instability. He was too clear-sighted to imagine that such a grouping was conceivable at that juncture. Finally he said with some irritation :

" That is seesaw politics."

To which Holstein retorted :

" Bismarck was perpetually shifting his position ! "

" Not like a weathercock ! " was Phili's retort.

Then Phili produced two letters, one from the Grand Duke of Baden, the other from the Grand Duke of Mecklenburg. They agreed in one point. " Things cannot go on as they are. Caprivi is ruining us."

Holstein had also brought a letter with him. It was from General von Verdy, who said :

" The public constantly emphasises the disinterestedness and honourable character of Caprivi and compares him in this respect favourably with Bismarck. They admit that he makes a lot of mistakes and cannot rise to great occasions. What will be left when they realise that his honour is a myth?"

This brought them to the subject of their midnight conclave—Caprivi.

Holstein had calculated correctly. The article in the *Kölnische Zeitung* had had its intended effect. Phili was convinced that Caprivi's hand had launched this attack against him. The Chancellor must go. Phili would do the necessary with the Kaiser. He fully approved of his Imperial master's sentiment:

"If anyone is in my way, I crush him."

The question now was: "Who is to be Chancellor?"

Holstein made a few suggestions. Phili listened attentively, hoping to hear his own name; but the Geheimrat appeared not even to consider it. Then the Count enquired whom the Conservatives had chosen as their candidate. He thought he knew, through his reporter von Helldorff-Bedra—jestingly known as "the bad general with no troops," because he was always founding useless parties with no adherents—that the Conservative party had yesterday chosen him, Philip Eulenburg. Holstein looked at him in surprise. "The Conservatives? Oh, their nominee is Zedlitz."

Phili got an ugly shock.

He was even more alarmed at the name of the candidate than at his own rejection.

" Zedlitz ? Ye Gods ! You can't trust anyone. That's the end of Helldorff," he reflected.

A servant from the Castle to seek the Count : " Everyone is anxiously awaiting the coming of the guest. The kitchen folk are in despair."

Holstein was quite unmoved. His compliments to the Countess. He preferred to remain in the forest.

Then, as if he had just guessed the other's possible thought :

" It would be a great mistake to aim at the Chancellorship yourself yet awhile, Phili. You have not yet the requisite official seniority : nor the experience. Premature success of that sort only makes bad blood. It provokes jealousy and discontent. And the Emperor would be the first to suffer."

Philip Eulenburg, ever impulsive :

" No, never ! My Imperial friend is vastly more to me than my ambition."

" I have spoken quite openly to you," concluded Holstein, " for in my experience no one ever forgives you for mistakes you let him make."

Morning was breaking as Holstein drove to the station. Phili pleaded with him to stay the night at the Castle and not insist on travelling by this slow train that would stop for ages at every station, as it brought the morning milk cans to the city.

But all his host's entreaties were vain. The Geheimrat liked to be first in the office. And that was that.

At 12 o'clock noon the Kaiser signed the dismissal of his Imperial Chancellor, Count von Caprivi. Between the fish and the joint at lunch His Majesty said :

" I've had to get rid of Caprivi ; he was getting more and more impossible and wanted to bear-lead me all the time."

III. HOHENLOHE [1894—1900]

## 29

## FULL DRESS OPERA

IT was an evening in October. Frau von Lebbin was going to the Opera for the first time since her husband's death. She was décolletée, for the Emperor had commanded *théâtre paré*.

"If His Majesty really wants to see my nice old wrinkled back, why so he shall!" said she to Holstein, whom she met at Ewest's in response to his wish to see her beforehand.

He was amazed to see how young she looked out of mourning. He rearranged her flowers for her with a smile and said a little sadly:

"Ah, Lena, how old I feel to-night!"

There was a lively coming and going in front of the Opera House. Baron Marschall caught sight of Holstein as the latter was just turning in to the Charlottenstrasse on the way home. He hailed him. They turned and went back together to the stairs leading up to the Court circle, for Marschall was attending by royal command.

The Foreign Secretary put the Geheimrat *au courant* of the latest news:

"What ghastly days of Chancellor interregnum we are having! It almost looks as if Prince

Hohenlohe's chances were the brightest. But the Princess will certainly do her best to make him refuse any post in Berlin. She would prefer Paris or St. Petersburg, but she would like best of all to stay in Strassburg, where she is holding court like a vice-reine. She hates Prussia and she hates Berlin. I don't mind telling you in confidence—I had it myself direct from Mirbach—that the Empress had a telegram from her to-day from Strassburg, saying that she did not want to come to Berlin on any terms. Let us be thankful that in Prussia at least it is still the men who run politics. . . .

"As for Zedlitz: the Emperor is suddenly dead against his appointment. Count Phili isn't in the running; he is too hesitating, too soft for the job. Of course, he is amazingly gifted, but like all the Eulenburgs so infernally cautious. He would never adopt any line that held the remotest possibility of future unpleasantnesses for him. It rather looks as if he anticipated things of the kind, for he is lying very low."

"Good business," thought Holstein to himself.

"In spite of excellent qualifications, Bernhard Bülow is hardly mature enough. There is only Prince Hohenlohe left. His income in Strassburg is £10,000 a year, and the Chancellor's salary that Bismarck used to draw would give him only £3,000 or so in Berlin; not more. He's not rich enough to supplement out of his own private pocket so he'll probably refuse on that ground if not on any other. The Princess, of course, is immensely rich, but, as she will move heaven and earth to keep out of it, that hardly counts. The only possibility is that the Kaiser might offer Hohenlohe a substantial sum from the Emergency Fund to make good what he would lose by coming here. Anyhow, that was what I suggested to His Majesty to induce Hohenlohe to accept."

Servants were busily hurrying up the steps. The foyer below was filling with courtiers. A lackey burst in :

" His Imperial Majesty has just left the Palace ! "

It was too late for Holstein to make his escape. He was hemmed in on every side and an attempt to force a passage out might mean a collision with the Emperor. So he posted himself behind a pillar while Marschall lined up for the reception. Suddenly an unknown voice challenged him from the rear :

" Will you be kind enough to show your papers. I am a private detective on duty."

Holstein deigned only to turn his head slightly :

" That's all right. I am Geheimrat von Holstein of the Foreign Office."

The official detective, whose duties had always lain at Court, and who knew intimately the appearance of every attaché of the Foreign Office, was flummuxed. He had never heard this magic name, let alone seen its possessor. He was just about to remove Holstein when the Intendant General of the Royal Entertainments, armed with his long staff of office, happened to come by, and, recognising Holstein, held out his hand. This saved the Geheimrat from a distressing misadventure, for just at that moment the royal carriage drove up.

As if a magician's wand had conjured them up, the whole dazzling suite stood suddenly in the hall, the Emperor in their midst. He climbed the stairs slowly. In front of him, backwards up the steps, retreated the gorgeous multi-coloured line of Officers of the Household, Aides de Camp and Gentlemen in Waiting. The entire line of elderly men bowed as they achieved each fresh altitude. It was common knowledge that His Majesty much enjoyed this ceremony. So, laboriously, one step after another was mounted, until all that was seen from below was the twinkling of orders, the gleam of white waistcoats and the gold lace of court dress. Finally, the clinking of swords and daggers died away. Then a deafening fanfare announced the ruler's entry into the festive house.

Holstein gazed up the empty stair. " Mummery ! " he cried. " Theatricals in the theatre. What a blessing the old man didn't live to see it ! "

And he sadly took his lonely way to his home.

## 30

# HOLSTEIN WARNS HOHENLOHE

HOLSTEIN to Prince Hohenlohe. Berlin, 26th October, 1894. (Holograph letter.) A great patriotic duty awaits Your Serene Highness. I do not know of anyone except yourself competent to deal with the present dangers. Your name, your past, inspire a confidence such as no other statesman, except Fürst Bismarck himself, can pretend to.

Success depends entirely on your Highness's summoning to your side the right men for the various departments—for this reason I would beg your Highness to make no binding promises until we have taken counsel together.

One point I have already noted is that Marschall is indispensable. He is a first-rate debater. His knowledge of internal German affairs, particularly everything connected with constitutional law, mark him as one corner-stone of your *régime*. I just mention this because I know that people have been seriously intriguing against him with the Kaiser. As soon as I found this out I dropped a hint, some eight days ago, to Philip Eulenburg—giving him permission to make what use he liked of it—that if Marschall got his *congé* I should go too.

It is a matter of political life and death for your Highness to get Marschall into the Prussian Ministry of State as a makeweight to Miquel—a measure which so far Botho Eulenburg has always opposed.

But your Highness will have a number of other high offices to fill. I should recommend keeping, for a time at any rate, Geheimrat Günther, the present second Councillor, as chief of the Imperial Chancellery. I should then suggest Prince Alexander * as second, or, if he will not accept (which I should greatly regret), then Prince Ratibor * (Landrat). I do not know the latter personally, but he is said to be thoroughly sound. I keep wondering whether this stroke of Fate will not have its repercussions on the Russian question. Everything else when we meet.

I hardly need mention that I myself—if I remain at all—wish no alteration in my own position.

Ps.—Until we have had a chat your Highness will, I trust, not allow any single individual to establish a claim on you. I except Köller because you already know him personally. But do not definitely commit yourself till all the necessary personnel has been decided on.

* Son and nephew of Hohenlohe respectively.

130

On October 28, 1894, Prince Chlodwig zu Hohenlohe-Schillingsfürst became German Imperial Chancellor.

A nephew of his came attired in the official uniform of Adjutant to pay his respects. The uncle, indicating the formal dress, said :

" That you can drop. You are welcome to come to me at any time without formality. But one thing I would beg of you : when you go into Berlin society you will hear a lot about Holstein— incidentally a great deal that is most unjust—don't let yourself be drawn into conversation. I have known Holstein this thirty years ; I knew him even before the Paris episode. I know the worst —but I need the man."

## 31

## " I AM THE IMPERIAL CHANCELLOR "

WRITING once to Frau von Lebbin, from the Harz, Holstein said :
"You should read letters through, not once, but several times. They then give a totally different impression."

To anyone who reads this letter to Prince Hohenlohe according to Holstein's prescription a second meaning becomes clear, running between the lines and revealing his art in all its subtlety and glory. There is praise—not without blame ; self-confidence—not without anxiety ; advice, warning, threats, desires. For himself he wants no change of position, if any is attempted he threatens to resign. He is perfectly aware that *Kladderadatsch* was right in printing below a Holstein caricature :

"Bring the Slowworm into the light of day : it dies."

He knew that he would cut no advantageous figure in the public eye, therefore he intended to defend his subterranean citadel.

Nicknames were much to the fore at this period. The "Slowworm" got a letter from

Phili in which his new Chief figured as the
" Mummy." Bülow spoke of Philip Eulenburg
as " our Palace Lapdog," and of Holstein as the
" Marten," while Holstein alluded to Bülow as
the " Fox." The three interchanged these plea-
santries behind each other's backs, while out-
wardly they vied with each other in assurances of
friendship.

These assurances were most necessary, for
every moment brought fresh friction. Holstein
got perfectly wild with Phili. When the
Geheimrat had just got a promising intrigue
nicely going, Philip Eulenburg would blow in
from Vienna like a *deus ex machinâ* and patch
things up. Holstein would be in despair while
Eulenburg felt all the self-satisfaction that a
seemly and Christian act is wont to rouse in an
unsuspecting, kindly soul. This was the beginning of the first tension between Holstein and
Philip Eulenburg, on which time was later to
put so ugly a complexion.

The Mummy had taken up his quarters in
Berlin. From the first, Princess Hohenlohe made
no effort to conceal her aversion from the capital,
and she went straight from Strassburg to her
Russian estates.

Holstein was amazed at the calm decisiveness
of Hohenlohe's first orders. He perceived that
the Mummy was most confoundedly alive. The
two Bismarcks used to shout at the attendants, in

extremity would sometimes even set Tyras on them. Now all was dignified and quiet in the Foreign Office, as dignified as the Prince himself. With his markedly stooping figure, his fine-cut features, his cultured voice, his slight but expressive gestures, in harmony with his faultlessly tailored clothes, the Chancellor looked like the last of the grands seigneurs.

All the politicians of this period have been pulled to pieces and vilified. Every missile rebounds harmlessly from the utter straightness of this stooping man. His integrity is unassailable.

The Geheimrat soon noted with dismay that Hohenlohe might prove the stronger man. This suspicion became a certainty after a conversation during which Holstein forcibly pressed his own wishes and submitted to his Chief a draft merely for signature. The Prince's quiet reply was :

" You will not forget that it is I who am the Imperial Chancellor."

## 32

## COUPS D'ÉTAT

HOHENLOHE and Marschall were busy one day looking through the papers that had accumulated during the interregnum. They found a document with the heading: "Coups d'état of Count Caprivi and Count Botho Eulenburg." It was in Holstein's handwriting. The Chancellor glanced through the sheets and merely remarked:

"Quite absurd. But you see, Marschall, how dangerous the fellow is. Here are the Kaiser's initials on it. So he has seen it, too. This memorandum accounts for Caprivi's fall if I am not mistaken. We shall soon be back in the times of Frederick William II. and Bischoffs-werder!"

Marschall nodded affirmatively:

"Bismarck hit out and made the sparks fly, but with him you knew just how you stood. Holstein always works in the dark. Under him the Foreign Office has become a regular witches' kitchen!"

"That's the very word for it," laughed the Chancellor, "with Holstein as *maître d'hôtel!*"

To which Marschall replied:

"Yesterday one of the young secretaries, who at the moment is in high favour with Holstein, showed me a book in which the Geheimrat had written a few words by way of dedication. They ran something like this : ' A diplomat's stock-in-trade is not untruth, but the power to keep the truth from time to time in abeyance.' That's good ! " he added.

"Perhaps," said the Prince dubiously. " For my part, I have always lived up to Boileau's dictum :

" ' Rien n'est beau que le vrai ! ' "

## 33

### EX FLAMMIS ORIOR

THE Emperor had followed Marschall's advice and placed an additional £5,000 a year from the Emergency Fund at Hohenlohe's disposal. He assumed that this would anticipate an unspoken wish. The Chancellor had the habit, after glancing through any account to look at the final total, and say :

" Is that the lot ? Nothing more ? "

He did not know much about finance, but he was always a martinet in money matters, and tolerated no jesting on the subject. He respectfully refused the Kaiser's offer. When his service as Chancellor was over, his private budget showed a deficit of £25,000.

" Preferable to living on charity," he remarked to Prince Alexander.

Meantime, Holstein had heard of the Emperor's action. He was horrified that a private grant should be debited to the Emergency Fund. His sense of duty was at once in arms, but, as so often, he took the wrong means of dealing with the situation. He handed on the information for the Social Democrat party in the Reichstag to make public use of.

When he learned of Hohenlohe's magnanimous refusal of the proffered grant he remembered the proud motto of the house : *ex flammis orior !* * Assuredly the figure of this man was like a leaping flame which dominates and illumines the surrounding darkness.

* A play on the name Hohen-lohe (*leaping-flame*).

## 34

OLD PRUSSIA IS DONE FOR

HOLSTEIN was sorting his papers one evening—he used always to take the most important documents home with him—when a gentleman from the *Kreuzzeitung* was announced.

" Tell the gentleman that I will see him, but that I am sorely pressed for time."

The servant showed the untimely caller in.

Holstein could scarcely believe his eyes. His visitor was no less a person than the Editor-in-Chief of the *Kreuzzeitung*, Baron William von Hammerstein, member of the Reichstag.

" But, my dear Baron! Do sit down. I thought it was one of your reporters."

Hammerstein had dropped into an armchair. A convulsive sobbing shook the stately frame. Holstein could not imagine what could be the matter. One of the most respected members of the Conservative party behaving like a man in despair.

Then words broke from him singly, jerkily :

" Save me, Geheimrat, save me. I have swindled and committed forgery—I am a fugitive —For God's sake, give me a passport. It's nothing to you. A passport—for the love of heaven ! "

At first the Geheimrat failed to take it in. He sat at his table like a statue and stared in front of him. Then he said icily :

" I can issue you no passport. I should make myself an accessory after the fact. Be a man and face your trial. That is the only conduct worthy of a man of our caste and of Conservative convictions ! "

His visitor had completely lost his self-control ; he let himself go, begging and imploring to be given a passport, urging finally that the prestige of State and the Monarchy would suffer if the case were completely exposed.

Holstein turned his eyes full on him searchingly :

" That is precisely why you must stand your trial—for the sake of State and Monarchy. People like you who have helped to govern the country and have betrayed their trust, must take their punishment. It is the only way to save the State and the Monarchy in the eyes of posterity ! "

Later, when Holstein read the sentence :

" Three years' penal servitude," he smote his desk with the palm of his hand in the familiar gesture :

" Old Prussia is done for ! " said he.

## 35

### RESIGNATIONS

THE new Chancellor, Prince Hohenlohe, considered it courteous to pay a visit to his great predecessor in Friedrichsruh. It was a formal visit, a mere politeness which was approved on all sides, even by the Emperor.

Only Holstein, and he of course, felt outraged.

He heard that the Chancellor had breakfasted with Herbert Bismarck the day before, and that it was not beyond the bounds of possibility that Hohenlohe might consider it his mission to re-instate Bismarck in Wilhelmstrasse No. 76. The thought of a reconciliation between Bismarck and the Kaiser seemed so alarming that Holstein once again tendered his resignation.

It should here be mentioned that different estimates are current of the number of times that Holstein threatened to resign. Philip Eulenburg tots it up to eleven, Bülow only reckons four. Holstein did in fact send in eleven tenders of resignation, but only four of them got so far as the Kaiser. The others were held up by the various Chancellors or Secretaries of State and retracted after fresh explanations and reconciliations with the Geheimrat, so that both statements are correct. The rumour that Holstein resigned over twenty times is a myth.

The offer of resignation of February 1st, 1895, was couched in the following terms :

" Since it would appear that my continued presence at the Foreign Office is one among the obstacles to His Majesty's desired rapprochement to Fürst Bismarck, I consider it my duty to remove this obstacle from His Majesty's path. A second reason for an immediate resignation is supplied by the cataract trouble from which I am suffering, which would in any case compel my retirement at no very distant date.

" In these circumstances I would beg your Serene Highness graciously to take the steps necessary to permit my withdrawal from the Imperial service. I should like at the same time to emphasise that this request is prompted by an unalterable decision. Since my eyes have suffered in the service, I have a claim to the full legal pension.

" Finally, I should wish to express to your Highness my respectful and cordial thanks for the trust and goodwill with which your Highness has favoured me over a period of many years.

" Your Highness's

most humble, most obedient servant,

HOLSTEIN,

Wirklicher Geheimer Legationsrat."

The Chancellor's reply was immediate :

(Written in pencil. Draft only !)

142

" You yourself not so long ago urgently coun-
selled me to accept the Chancellorship. I did so
on your advice and relying on your assistance.
You would be breaking the bargain if you were
to retire now and leave me in the lurch. Present
conditions put a strain on all of us. It is up to us,
however, to defend the monarchy as such, and
put up with what cannot be altered. These conditions are distressing to you ; your going would
not make them less distressing, but would leave
me to bear the brunt alone. My visit to Bismarck
has roused your suspicions . . ."

At this point the draft breaks off.

The same day Prince Alexander Hohenlohe
called on Holstein at his father's instance. He
had first to acclimatise himself to the atmosphere
of the room, which was so thick that a newcomer
always found it oppressive.

Prince Alexander at once perceived that the
Geheimrat had taken counsel with himself during
the night, and was prepared to defend to the
death his position at his own desk ; that, in fact,
the slightest possible gesture of conciliation would
be enough to induce him to withdraw his resignation. He therefore made it clear that there was
not a thought of any reconciliation at the moment
between Bismarck and the Kaiser, that Bismarck
had not the slightest intention of returning, and,
finally, that the breakfast yesterday at Herbert's
had been a mere act of courtesy.

The Geheimrat's mind was set at rest. He stayed. When the son reported the interview to his father, the Chancellor said :

" Holstein is a most extraordinary fellow. He often recalls to me Goethe's phrase in the West-östlicher Divan ' Dass Du nicht enden kannst das macht Dich gross ! ' " *

A few weeks later Otto von Bismarck celebrated his eightieth birthday in Friedrichsruh. The German Reichstag refused to send congratulations. On which Holstein's comment was :

" Bismarck deserved better of them than that ! But indeed the swine don't deserve to be allowed to offer him congratulations ! "

The Emperor and Hohenlohe both attended the festivities. Holstein heard that General von Bronsart had also been in attendance. Now he knew that the General was strongly suspected of trying, in season and out of season, to bring about a reconciliation between His Majesty and the aged ex-Chancellor.

Holstein tendered yet another resignation.

It was his seventh.

* It is your staying power that makes you great.

## THE BATH-PROPRIETOR

**D**URING these months the influence of
Count Philip Eulenburg increased to such
an extent that it became almost impossible
to approach the Kaiser except through him. It
was an open secret that the Emperor was completely under his spell, and that he was a daily
guest at the Palace. By express command Phili
might come in whenever he liked, merely announced by the Adjutant on duty, and this at a
time when the Ministers were all complaining
that His Majesty was inaccessible and would
scarcely find time to hear their official reports.

Philip Eulenburg's rise filled Holstein with misgiving. He saw his former pupil escaping his
leading-strings and carving out his own career
independently of his quondam patron. He felt
wounded. But he felt even more enraged that
this Ambassador should so calmly leave his Austrian post—to which Holstein had appointed him
—and spend his time playing the charmer at Court
while unread files accumulated in piles in his
office in Vienna. It seemed to him that Phili
sorely needed some firm anchorage of duty if his
gifts and his genius were to be really useful to the

State. And the Kaiser was no less in need of similar discipline. If these two dreamers were to try their hands at the higher flights of statecraft. . . . Holstein wrung his hands. . . . Ye Gods ! Where would it end ?

A deadly enemy of Philip Eulenburg's came to see Holstein about this time, a certain Count Dohna, also an East Prussian by origin. He and Phili had been at school together at the Hintertragheim in Königsberg, had been fellow-students at the University, and had remained friends until Dohna had introduced Philip Eulenburg at Court. Since that time in 1886 their friendship had broken down because Dohna, who considered that he had launched Eulenburg, could not repress his envy and jealousy at Phili's success and Phili's superiority. This galled him the more that he had been unable to make good himself. So his friendship turned to hate, and he now came to bring some welcome news to Holstein.

Philip Eulenburg had once confided to him that he was being blackmailed by a certain bathproprietor and had had to pay him £3,000 at various times to buy his silence. Holstein's plan was soon formed.

The Geheimrat made an exception for once and accepted an invitation of Prince Hohenlohe's, mastering even his objection to the foreign hostess merely in order to meet Phili in the presence of witnesses. It was to be a beer-party, a form of entertainment going back to the Bismarck tradition. Holstein skilfully manœuvred the Chancellor and Phili into a corner and engineered a conversation. Then he related a case of political blackmail which he had once come across when he was Bismarck's secretary, and opined that one could never be rigorous enough in dealing with such people.

A little liquor always went to Philip Eulenburg's head—a weakness which Harry von Arnim had also suffered from. He volunteered his own experience with the bath-proprietor. Holstein hastened home to put it down in writing.

Next morning he looked in at the Police Headquarters and gave the President a glimpse at his protocol. When the President saw the names of the witnesses : Count Dohna, the senior of his house, Prince Hohenlohe, Imperial Chancellor, and Geheimrat von Holstein of the Foreign Office, he had no hesitation in making a note of the data in his archives. Holstein asked for a confirmation of the fact that this document would now be on the police records, and got it without more ado. The same day he had an interview with the Chancellor and asked permission to make an entry about Philip Eulenburg's conversation of yesterday on the confidential personal file. Rather wearily, as was his wont, Hohenlohe asked :

" Do you think that's necessary ? "

Whereupon Holstein promptly trotted out his paper from the President of Police :

L 2

" I'm very much afraid so, your Highness," he said with a sigh. " Unfortunately, the whole affair is well known to the Police. I have their official confirmation here."

Whereupon Hohenlohe, to whom such subjects were highly repugnant, signed the document.

Holstein now held Philip Eulenburg in the hollow of his hand. " If Phili by chance has a mind to dance, I can pipe a pretty little tune for him ! "

## 37

## OLD HANNA

FRAU VON LEBBIN greeted her friend one afternoon with : "Do you know who's turned up, Fritz ? Old Frau Hanna from Schwedt. She looked you up in the city and got my address there and came on here. She is outside in the kitchen."

Holstein sat down for a chat with his old nurse. She was the only survivor of the three women who had been round him as a child when his father died. In the joy of meeting they forgot the world at large, the kitchen, and the changes life had brought them both. The old woman reminded him how he had been nearly drowned as a boy in the pond on the estate, how he had been locked into the pantry when he was stealing goodies ; she chattered on about his father, his mother and his sister. The talk awakened all his old memories of the house with the walnut trees ; the door on to the steps with the coloured panes which made the world look all orange and blue and red ; old Chasseur, long since dead, with whom he used to romp ; he could feel again the well-remembered perfume of the old cupboards, the smell of the old home, again could hear the stairs creak and the old clocks strike the hour. She reminded him of his mother's guinea-fowl which used to make such a noise, of the spring that murmured and gleamed up like silver to greet him when he looked down out of the attic that he slept in as a lad—" the boys' attic " as they called it. He heard again the cuckoos calling and the frogs croaking in the park, the tooting of the tugs on the Oder, the trumpets of the Dragoons, and now and then a shriek from Mamselle in the kitchen when Chasseur had stolen something from her larder. A whole epoch which he had almost forgotten was conjured into life again.

When Frau von Lebbin put her head into the kitchen some time later they were still deep in talk—old Hanna with her wrinkled hand laid on " her boy's," while he was listening to her like a child and interrupting now and again with little cries—" How jolly that was, too ! " or, more sadly—" That's all over, now."

When she was going she kissed him on the forehead. " God bless you, Master Fritz ! " And the Geheimrat remained standing in the kitchen with a tear rolling down his cheek into the white beard. With it a load of fifty years rolled off his heart. It was the first time since his mother's death that anyone had kissed him—and the last.

## 38

## AUGUST EULENBURG

IT has already been mentioned how deeply Holstein feared the Master of the Household, August Eulenburg.* Here is a highly characteristic letter about this opponent of his.

*Thursday,*
*10th Feb., 1895—evening.*

To Prince Hohenlohe.

[He has explained that it would be impossible on official and legal grounds to confer the title of Minister of State on August Eulenburg and then continues] : " We are here dealing with an attempted *coup* the chief aim of which is to injure your Highness in the public eye and to make you appear a *chancellier fainéant* who just lets things drift. I could be eloquent in my anger about the *canaille* who have hatched the scheme, but out of consideration for your Highness's valuable time I shall be as brief as possible. I beg to advise your Highness to summon the Ministers of State to a confidential meeting—not to a regular council—at 10 a.m. if possible, and put this question to them :

---

* August and Botho Eulenburg were brothers, cousins of " Phili's " father.

'Gentlemen, I have a serious concrete reason for asking your opinion on the following point : Is it possible to confer the title of Minister of State on a gentleman who is in fact a Privy Councillor (Wirklicher Geheimer Rat), but who has never actually been a Minister of State ? And, if so, what preliminary formalities are necessary ? '

If they say ' yes ' so much the better. If—which is more probable—they answer in the negative, then your Highness can lay their opinion before His Majesty with all speed, preferably through the same channel as that through which the proposal reached you. If His Majesty has been so indiscreet as already to sign the document conferring the title, he must just contrive somehow to get it suppressed. Has Lucanus so far committed himself that his name is known as the originator of the suggestion ? That would be useful. But your Highness must lose no time ! To-morrow morning early ! "

The Chancellor shook his head as he read this missive.

"What babies they all are ! " he said, as he relegated it to a pile of other warnings and wishes of Holstein's.

## 39

# THE ARMY

HOLSTEIN summoned Hatzfeld to Berlin. He wanted a chat with this most trustworthy of all his tools, for he needed someone to whom he could pour out his woes. The Army was the subject of his most acute anxiety. They were letting it fall to pieces. "As Bismarck once said," began Holstein,

'The Army is the branch on which we are all perched. Anyone who lays the axe to it is my enemy!'

"The Army is the most valuable factor in foreign politics and here I see it being frittered away, misused for all sorts of frivolous purposes. We are working up to another 1806.* A phrase is going the rounds of the Casinos in Potsdam which is of course meant as a jest, but which conceals an alarming truth : 'We have one regiment of foot, we have one regiment of horse, and there is a rumour that we have some armed rabble in the provinces.' It is only too true that the Guards, and more recently the Marines, are the only regiments to which His Majesty pays the

* The Prussians were defeated by Napoleon at Jena and Auerstedt in 1806.

slightest attention, so that great discontent is felt throughout the rest of the Army. The Kaiser constantly parades about in the uniforms of the 1st regiment of Guards—which he calls ' the First Regiment in Christendom '—and the leather tunic of the Garde du Corps. It's not right. Trifling like this is not the way to keep up the stern old Prussian spirit of the Army.

" They tell me that His Majesty spends hours designing new hanging cords like some he took a fancy to in Russia and which he wants to introduce. So as to be able to wear them himself he has appointed himself Adjutant-General to his grandfather, William the Great of immortal memory. If the old man could hear the title he would turn in his grave.

" With it all, the Kaiser's intentions are of the best. He means no harm. He wastes his time over such childish toys only because his entourage like to see him busy at play so that they can get the reins into their own hands.

" If once His Majesty becomes aware of this— and he is very sensitive to slights or neglect—he will fling himself heart and soul into serious work. But then it will not be possible for me to keep an eye on the whole chessboard of foreign politics.

" He dashes off letters without consulting any- one, without even telling anyone, letters to monarchs and ministers, to foreign officers and to the Tsar—so that we are confronted with one crisis after another."

While Holstein was thus holding forth, Hatzfeld had been anxiously observing his friend. He could not help noticing that he looked much older and that his sight had grown markedly worse. When he reached out to take up the ruler as he was talking, he often missed it.

Holstein went on:

" I know nothing about internal politics and don't want to. But yesterday I found a telegram on the Chancellor's desk which the Kaiser had despatched from Hohenfinow; it really is the limit. It is about the Revolutionary Bill which the Reichstag has just thrown out. His Majesty wires ' Many thanks for the news. So we've still got the fire hose for every day use and grapeshot up our sleeve for special occasions ! ' And this telegram comes, if you please *en clair*, my dear Hatzfeld, not even in cypher.

" Hohenlohe told me that the Kaiser once said about the Reichstag: ' If those fellows don't come to heel I'll send for them to the Palace and tell them what I think of them—at some length, too ! ' Whereupon the Chancellor took occasion to call His Majesty's attention in writing to the existence of the Constitution. It is a first-class letter ; Hohenlohe's letters are always forceful and to the point, and full of the most delicate humour, though he is a complete failure as a speaker.

" The relationship between the Kaiser and the Chancellor is very odd. Sometimes when the

Kaiser is in a good humour with him he calls him
' My dear Uncle,' * and a little later, when he is
annoyed, he reverts to the severely formal ' Highness.' Hohenlohe manages him splendidly, however, and drives him to work while he gently and
indulgently confiscates one toy after another.

" The people in high office are all running
round wringing their hands and prophesying evil
like Cassandra, and feeling quite jumpy over the
cynical and—unfortunately—all too pertinent
attacks of *Zukunft* and *Kladderadatsch*.

" People keep repeating that the Emperor has
a touch of genius and Philip Eulenburg is a genius
through and through. I don't question it, but
wasn't it Schopenhauer who said : ' Genius lives
just one storey higher than madness ! ' And this
insanity threatens to wreck the Empire for us.
History will cast it in our teeth that we paid more
heed to Imperial day-dreams than to the genuine
interests of the country. I care more for the
latter myself. You and I must do our best to get
the Kaiser to develop his own better qualities ; I
am sure that it is still perfectly possible. We must
try to prevent this mortal from making the most
immortal fool of himself. If we don't succeed,
then we must down him before he downs the
country."

* Hohenlohe was related to the Empress through her mother,
Princess Adelaide of Hohenlohe-Langenburg (see note p. 205).

## 40

## THE TAUSSIG LETTERS

THE German Ambassador, Bernhard von Bülow, had gone away on his summer leave and the Palazzo Caffarelli was closed; the whole of Rome was holidaying at Frascati or Rocca di Papa, and even Italian politics were having a rest. The Bülows were temporarily quartered in Berlin, partly in order to put in an appearance at the Foreign Office and to visit friends, partly to negotiate with Count Botho Wedel about one of his country places in Nordeney which they wanted to rent. As usual, they stayed at the Hotel Bristol.

Frau von Bülow issued an invitation to an " evening-dress tea-party," an invention of her own. This was a tea supplemented by cold dishes and punch, which often lasted on into the night, without, however, turning into a regular supper party.

Donna Maria von Bülow had been a pupil of Liszt and also of Hans von Bülow, long before she ever dreamt that she would one day bear that name herself. So it happened that these teas of hers were always diversified by musical items. This would normally have been an extra inducement to Holstein to stay away, for music to him was just so much unnecessary noise. But on this occasion he attended—for he wanted Bülow. There was a crowd of people of both sexes standing about in the reception room, which was crowded with baskets of flowers. These were all presents and offerings from people anxious to curry favour with the husband. Holstein saw Bernhard in the centre of a group and heard his jovial talk, always just a shade didactic, though amusing and full of witty sallies. He used to rest one hand between the buttons of his coat while the other, with a lively play of gesture, reinforced the effect of whatever he was saying at the moment.

Holstein had only once seen such skilful acting, that was Possart's at the Court Theatre in Munich in 1871. Frau von Bülow was going about amongst her guests, smiling the whole time, which did not, in fact, improve her appearance. She was no longer young and, as is so often the case with Italian women, she had aged quickly, and the reminders of her past beauty emphasised its loss. She sought to make good the deficiency by her vivacity and charm.

Several thick volumes in red morocco with gold lettering were being handed round. They were the works of Liszt, with dedications to the hostess. Then the central lights were switched off and lace-shaded standard lamps supplied the soft illumination for the concert.

During one of the intervals the proprietor of the Bristol Hotel strolled in, a small, stout man, the indefatigable host who knows everything and boasts his friendships with reigning princes. He brought in some new guests and introduced them. The Bülows' hospitality was renowned. Then the concert proceeded.

Late that night, long after the guests had all gone home, Frau von Bülow discovered to her horror that a little Venetian casket which stood on the chimney piece had vanished. They rang for the servants, made enquiries, the casket was gone.

The Ambassador was furious when he learnt that it had contained old love letters from his wife to Taussig, her music master, and his replies. There was no lack of mutual recrimination in the Hotel Bristol that night. They ran their minds over all the guests, trying to imagine who could possibly have stolen the letters, but all were people with whom they had been friends for years.

She was the first to exclaim : " Holstein ! "

" Inconceivable ! " was his retort.

But when his wife talked of " that terrifying man " and recalled the horror she had experienced when crossing the Tiergarten alone with him, Bülow decided to seek Holstein out at cockcrow.

The Geheimrat was still lying in his iron bed

and just pondering how he could get even with Hohenlohe, who had not deigned to answer him about the August Eulenburg business, when Röberchen whispered through the crack of the door that some Herr von Bülow was without.

The conversation dragged a little at first, for Bülow had some hesitation in formulating so grave an accusation, and Holstein was determined not to understand what on earth could have brought Bernhard round at this unholy hour, especially as he well knew his habit of lingering over breakfast.

Bülow gradually worked the conversation round to the loss of the casket. He saw Holstein blinking in his peculiar way, misunderstood the significance of this, lost his temper and flung an accusation of treachery in his face. Holstein adjusted the pillow at his back, took his pince-nez and looked straight at his visitor :

" I shall send you a challenge ! Now I must get up."

Bülow could not make up his mind to go at this point. He felt he had probably done Holstein an injustice, so he sat down at the writing desk in the next room and wrote a note asking permission to look him up in his office at noon.

Undisturbed by the exciting events of the morning, the Geheimrat was deep in his office work when a gentleman, a lieutenant, was announced

to see him. This person offered Holstein the
letters that had passed between Taussig and Maria
von Bülow, and named £250 as his price. Holstein remembered having seen this young man
last night in the Hotel Bristol during one of the
intervals. He took the letters. As soon as he
had them in his hand he asked the young man's
regiment.

"You will hear all that is further necessary
from your commanding officer," he said.

"His Excellency the Spectre" was rather different from the man the young lieutenant had
pictured. He saw himself probably cashiered.
As he turned to go, Holstein called him back.

"Have you a signet ring? Good. Be so kind
as to seal this packet of letters here and now."

When Bülow appeared at 12 o'clock, Holstein
handed him the sealed packet.

"A young officer, who is in debt, came just
now and offered me these as a weapon against
you! I want no weapon, least of all this one,
for you are a friend whom I trust and hope soon
to have at my side."

That afternoon the Ambassador, Bernhard von
Bülow, was paying a call on Frau von Lebbin,
for whom he had a great respect, which lasted
undiminished until her death in 1915. They
happened to speak of Holstein, and the lady
said :

" As an official, Fritz may be a difficult and disagreeable colleague, but as a person he is the most chivalrous and honourable man I know. No one knows him as I do ! "

## 41

# THE KRUGER TELEGRAM

AT the levée held at the Palace for the New Year, 1896, the Kaiser drew Prince Hohenlohe aside and spoke with irritation about England. He would like to see military measures taken against her in South Africa.

" That would mean war, your Majesty," was the Chancellor's reply.

He had scarcely recovered from the shock of this crazy suggestion, for he could see that Germany had none but the most subordinate interests in Cape Colony, when the Kaiser came round one day to the Palace of the Imperial Chancellor and again pressed for vigorous steps to be taken.

As a sort of safety-valve, to forestall something more serious, the Chancellor finally took the advice of Marschall and of the Colonial Director at the Foreign Office and gave his consent to the Emperor's sending a telegram to Ohm Kruger to serve as an indirect warning to England.

Holstein had some suspicion of what was in the air, but at the critical moment he was nowhere to be found. He had no mind to share the responsibility for the telegram : he was far-sighted enough to realise the dangerous possibilities

M 2

with which it was charged. On the other hand, he would not be sorry to see it prove the ruin of Marschall. Let the telegram go by all means ! But he would keep clear of it himself.

Meanwhile, he was sitting hiding in an attic with an attaché, and he at once wrote a letter to Philip Eulenburg which was indirectly intended for His Majesty's eye. Whenever he wanted anything to reach the Emperor he now sent it through Phili. This produced the anomalous situation that the most responsible director of Germany's foreign policy in Berlin could only get into touch with the Emperor *viâ* Vienna— because he himself had avoided making the royal acquaintance.

What lay behind this letter was this :

Minor differences apart, Marschall and Holstein had contrived to pull together admirably as colleagues, but Holstein wanted to get Bülow to Berlin and could only achieve his end by causing the fall of Marschall, whom Hohenlohe was sure to support. The impelling motive for the letter, however, was annoyance at Marschall's recent alliance with the Centre Party, whom Holstein always thought of as a pack of wicked Jesuits. His skilled pen used all its resources of shrewdness and cunning to produce the desired reaction in the Emperor. He wound up by saying that it was inconceivable that a Foreign Secretary could have been short-sighted enough to fire off a telegram which would explode like a bomb in England. If he (Holstein) had been consulted, he would never have permitted its despatch; he was far too well aware of His Majesty's wisdom and foresight to suppose that *he* could have wished to subject England to such an insult. No doubt His Majesty had acted under duress.

Holstein accurately reckoned that before his letter travelled round to the Imperial addressee the storm across the Channel would have burst and would have made a deep impression on the Kaiser.

English indignation about the Kruger telegram was wholehearted. The Press stormed against Emperor and Chancellor, called the act a shocking piece of tactlessness and a gross interference in matters which were no concern of Germany's, an act which imperilled the good relations between the two countries.

The Kaiser clearly recognised that Holstein's view, as expressed in the letter to Phili, was the right one. The flattery he swallowed whole, and he did not hesitate to make a scapegoat of Marschall.

Holstein, in a second letter *via* Vienna and Phili, advised that Marschall should be dismissed with all speed so as to make a good impression in England.

Three days later the Kaiser gave an audience to Colonel Schele, whom he had designated as a Chief of Staff, intending to follow up his telegram by sending him to Ohm Kruger and the Boers. The Colonel was now informed, to his amazement, that circumstances had in the meantime occurred which made the former plan inoperative, and he was now commissioned to draw up a plan of campaign for the English troops. This plan could then be sent as a sop to outraged Grandmama in England. Only at the last moment was the Emperor prevented from solemnly handing over this remarkable document to the English military attaché.

On this 8th of January Holstein's entry in his Diary ran :

" There is nothing to be done but tack to and fro between Scylla and Charybdis. This living from hand to mouth is most exhausting."

## 42

# HOLSTEIN DECLINES

NOTHING could give a better insight into the growing friction between Holstein and Philip Eulenburg than a letter of the latter's to Prince Hohenlohe, dated the 1st of March, 1897.

"Friend Holstein has bombarded me with such excited letters and telegrams—on the one side full of bitterness against His Majesty and on the other of distrust for Goluchowski—that I have been unable to preserve complete calm. I really had, for once, to tell him straight out just what I thought. And now he has so twisted the affair that he reads into my vexation the belief that I have lost patience with the political tangles His Majesty has been creating. This is far from the fact, but it is of course *une manière de voir les choses*.

"I would therefore beg your Highness not to interpret that letter of mine too seriously. You will easily believe that a long series of private telegrams from Holstein can goad a person into a retort in self-defence—in spite of the friendship that we all feel for him."

To which the Chancellor, with his unfailing wisdom and tolerance, replied :

BERLIN,
*March 3rd*, 1897.

" I can quite understand the state of irritation which our friend's letters and telegrams produced and cannot grudge you your ' retort.' On the other hand, we must not take amiss Holstein's moods of dissatisfaction. We must realise that he belongs essentially to the old Bismarck *régime*, under which everything was weighed and decided in the dingy ground-floor room of the Chancellor's Palace, and the monarch took good care not to interfere with Bismarck's doings. Now there has come along a young and eager master lusting for action, who is determined to put his finger into every pie, and creates confusion in the Embassies by the discrepancy between his personal utterances and the pronouncements of the Foreign Office, and even between what he himself says to one ambassador and to another. A diplomat of the old school cannot readily reconcile himself to this. Besides, Holstein does not know the Kaiser and so is insensible to the charm of His Majesty's personality which commands our sympathy and tolerance."

The echo to this letter was an announcement, through Philip Eulenburg, that the Kaiser graciously invited himself to a lunch at the

Chancellor's, and that he expressly wished Holstein also to be a guest. Holstein declined the invitation on the plea of indisposition.

The Emperor did not, however, give up the hope of at last making " the Spectre's " personal acquaintance. He despatched a servant during lunch to see whether Holstein was in the office. He was at work there right enough, but sent a note specifying his complaint and saying that he was not well enough to come.

As the Emperor was in the hall taking his leave, he said to Hohenlohe, in that delightfully easy way of his :

" No, please, you must not come out with me. It is bitterly cold. Give my greetings to Holstein and say from me that if he really has diarrhœa, I strongly recommend hot negus. It is a trusty Hohenzollern remedy ! "

## 43

## ARNIM AGAIN!

IT was an evening in June, 1897. Prince Alexander Hohenlohe had gone back to his study to fetch something he had forgotten. He was wearing evening dress, and the domestic order of the Hohenlohes sparkled on his breast. He had been invited with his father to the Palace to-night. Someone came shuffling along the corridor. The Prince wondered who it could be, opened the door, and saw: Holstein. The Geheimrat had been startled by hearing a noise in the deserted building and now entered the room where he had so often sat talking to Herbert Bismarck.

It struck him how strange a coincidence it was that two Bismarcks should be succeeded by two Hohenlohes, and that these men whom he had advised, almost controlled, might be succeeded by himself and Bernhard Bülow. Prince Alexander seemed to divine his thought:

"You know, of course, that Marschall is resigning? He has officially given his health as a pretext, but the truth is he does not feel his position secure since the Kaiser has dropped Bötticher, and the Reichstag are going to vote for the retention of § 270 of the Military Punishments Bill.* My father"—and as he spoke he squashed the stub of his cigarette into the ashtray—"is representing to His Majesty that if Marschall goes he also will ask leave to retire. The work is getting rather much for him, anyhow. This seems a suitable moment to make his exit!"

Holstein started: this was unforeseen. This was much too soon! He was just going to try to make sure whether the candidates whom the Chancellor would put forward were such as he would choose, when Prince Alexander himself continued:

"My father is thinking of proposing Bernhard Bülow as Imperial Chancellor. It isn't certain who would be Secretary of State for Foreign Affairs. Probably the Kaiser will want Philip Eulenburg! Someone at the Club yesterday said to me that His Majesty was considering Herbert Bismarck as a possibility. That would be quite conceivable, for the wind is in a better quarter in Friedrichsruh just now. The only person who would be against it is old Fürstin Johanna, who is too resentful and revengeful to find such a reconciliation easy to swallow."

Just then the orderly came in to announce that the carriage was at the door. The Prince did not notice how the Geheimrat tottered at this last item of news. It bowled him over; back in his own quarters he broke down. Phili or Herbert!

* Establishing the publicity of Courts Martial.

Impossible ! And Bülow : Chancellor at one leap —without having first been Secretary of State ! That would be the end !

What was to be done ? This very evening, so the Prince had said, the Chancellor was going to talk things over with the Kaiser—without *him*— without seeking *his* advice. The Emperor would gladly acquiesce in the appointment of the " excellent and admirable Bülow " as Chancellor, and rejoice in the idea of having friend Phili more closely attached to his person, and getting rid at one swoop of old Uncle Hohenlohe and boring old Marschall. Not a moment to lose ! He dashed home. Hauled out his frock coat. Ye Gods, when had he last worn it ! It reeked of camphor and moth ball. Röberchen fled to the chemist's back-door to fetch some lavender. Then he called a cab—" To the Palace ! " The driver anxiously looked round. It might be some madman. He had often read in the papers of lunatics wanting to be driven to the Palace because they thought they were some relation of the Kaiser's. It must be something of the kind, for his fare looked wilder every moment and grew more and more excited as he insisted that he must be driven to the Palace at once.

The N.C.O. at Entrance No. 4 felt no less doubtful about opening his brazen gate, for the untimely visitant had something uncanny about him. At last the officer of the watch came along and admitted him. Holstein must see the Chancellor at once. This was not possible : their Majesties were still at table.

Holstein sat down on a stool in the guard-room while the grenadiers slept round him on the benches and a lieutenant at the table sat writing a report. A mixed smell of leather, brass and tobacco seemed to stifle him. At last the meal upstairs was over. He was ushered into an adjutant's room on the first floor. He at once felt that things weren't going to be as easy here as over there in the Wilhelmstrasse. The Adjutant on duty " greatly regretted," and a Gentleman in Waiting explained that they could not take Holstein straight to the Chancellor, for he was at the moment actually in conversation with His Majesty.

That was just what Holstein had come to prevent. He must get in, if it cost the half of the kingdom. So in desperation he begged, if he could not at once gain access to the Chancellor, that they should kindly announce him to His Majesty. No one liked to take this responsibility, but they fetched out the Gentleman in Waiting who was to-day doing duty for the Master of the Household. The Geheimrat did not recognise him.

The more Holstein explained and implored, threatened and insisted, the calmer the other became. Finally he shrugged his shoulders with some impatience and remarked in a hoarse and haughty voice as he twisted the cord of his monocle between his fingers :

" I am very sorry, Geheimrat, that I am not in a position to accede to your request. You have always—at your own urgent desire—avoided presenting yourself at Court. You will understand that I must refer you to the usual channels : to-morrow and every day the list for people desiring audiences lies open from eleven to one, you only need duly to enter your name on it and announce yourself to me, Count Arnim, Gentleman in Waiting ! "

With a formal bow he disappeared behind the lofty, white folding-doors.

The all-powerful Geheimrat gazed speechlessly after him. Here, indeed, his power ended.

Silently he descended the stairs ; glass doors opened for him and closed behind him. He noticed nothing. He reflected only how systematically he had refused to share the pleasures of this Court and now, in the moment of deadly need, he was turned away. An immense bitterness flooded his soul ; above all an immense disgust, a longing to be done with it all.

Weary and inert, he again took his seat on the stool in the guard-room, determined to have a word with the Chancellor on his way home. But the emotions of the day had exhausted him. He fell asleep. He dreamt of Russia. He saw the white epaulettes of the Alexander Regiment gleaming round him, he dreamt of the Neva and the days of thirty years ago, of Alexander, of

To-day and the anxieties of To-morrow. And the Geheimrat's white head pillowed itself on the rude table where not many moments ago a Pomeranian grenadier had been cutting up his bread and cheese. Upstairs the Gentleman in Waiting was proudly swaggering round:

" I gave it to the blighter in the neck ! " said Arnim's son, as he threw himself, laughing, into an armchair.

About midnight a sudden signal woke Holstein with a start. The sound of short trotting, clatter, a carriage driving up on rubber-tyred wheels, " Guard, turn out ! " A roll of drums. Prince Hohenlohe was driving out across the inner court. Too late !

In despair old Holstein dragged himself home through the darkened city. He could not sleep. An incubus was on his chest, a long dark shadow from the corner where the iron safe was standing. It threatened to stifle him.

" Arnim," he groaned with effort. Holstein was delirious.

## 44

## BÜLOW BECOMES SECRETARY OF STATE FOR FOREIGN AFFAIRS

HOLSTEIN'S mind was made up. He would go. Once already this year (1897), on the 17th of June, he had handed the Chancellor his resignation on account of an infamous article of Harden's, but Hohenlohe had been able to persuade him to remain.

The agreement about Kiaochow was in preparation. Holstein was dead against it and could see no good omen in it for the future. All the better to retire and evade the responsibility. Then came the news that the Kaiser, contrary to everyone's expectations, intended to retain Hohenlohe as Chancellor, make Bülow Secretary of State for Foreign Affairs and leave Philip Eulenburg in Vienna. A telegram from Kiel, where the Emperor had gone to hold a Naval Review, brought confirmation. That comforted the Geheimrat : he stayed on.

On taking office, Bülow immediately paid an official visit to his predecessor, Baron Marschall. He felt at once that the pain caused to this admirable man by his supersession could most effectively be eased by appointing him to some dignified and congenial post. The selection of a suitable billet was not easy, for Marschall could speak neither French nor English well. Bülow, however, promised him Constantinople.

The new Foreign Secretary found his Chief, Prince Hohenlohe, in a large easy chair, weak and old and more than ever stooped. The bluish veins stood out on the aged hand which was caressing a tan-coloured dachshund.

As soon, however, as the Chancellor began, almost in a whisper, to expound the situation, Bülow found that his mental powers were unimpaired. He was as wise as ever and as full of insight, with the same calm, well-balanced appreciation of aims to be pursued and forces to be reckoned with.

Bülow then went on to Holstein's :

" Just a few more years to wait, you and I," whispered the Geheimrat, " and then you will have the position that is yours by right—the Imperial Chancellorship."

That evening's *Kladderadatsch* brought out a front-page cartoon in which Hohenlohe, in the background, hobbles off the scene on crutches, while in the foreground Bülow strikes a pose on a rostrum at the base of which Holstein crouches as prompter.

Mephistopheles had found his Faust.

## 45

## THE RIGHT TO TELEGRAPH

AT the very beginning of their joint term as colleagues Bülow and Holstein fell seriously foul of each other. First the Geheimrat chose to give credence to a current rumour that Bülow proposed to make Jacobi chief of his Press department. This would have been contrary to their understanding, and in any case Holstein had not even been consulted. So, though Bülow's office was next door to his, he wrote a threatening letter to him and insisted that this intention should be abandoned, otherwise he himself would feel compelled to resign. The tone of this communication was not at all to Bülow's taste, so he went round to Holstein and tried to explain that after all it was he who was Secretary of State. On the Geheimrat's desk he caught sight of two draft telegrams, one addressed to Hatzfeld, the other to Radolin. He waited a couple of days; neither of the telegrams was submitted to him. He took occasion to have a talk with Prince Hohenlohe about Holstein's private telegrams. It would become practically impossible to maintain any unity of policy if the Secretary of State did not know what instructions had been issued—for the telegrams could only have been about questions of foreign policy.

Hohenlohe, in his tired voice, explained the situation in a word or two :

" It is perfectly true.   Bismarck, unfortunately, gave Holstein permission to despatch private telegrams direct to the heads of embassies on his own responsibility.   They may be sent in cypher, but they need not be registered, and they bear the word ' Private ' !   I should strongly advise you not to attempt to rob Holstein of his toy. It would make him bitter as well as angry.   So you see already, my dear fellow, that life is none too easy for us in ' The Office ' here—especially where Holstein is concerned ! "

Bülow was much depressed.   It was plain enough that the Geheimrat was only carrying on a practice sanctioned by Bismarck, but this dual control had got to stop once for all.   His vanity could not tolerate Holstein as a sort of overseer. There was only one remedy—for Prince Hohenlohe was not prepared to interfere—to let the Kaiser know in the course of conversation how the matter stood, and induce him to cancel Holstein's right to send private telegrams.

When Bülow had gone, Hohenlohe said to his son :

" Do you know, Alexander, I'm afraid Bülow is accustomed only to well-trained dogs.   He must be careful, or he'll find that alert watchdog Holstein biting him in the leg ! "

179

N 2

## 46

## SONGS OF THE ROSE

**A**N urgent telegram from Bülow brought Philip Eulenburg to Berlin. Phili anticipated nothing agreeable. His first visit was to the Foreign Office. There was no one left when he arrived except Holstein, who was just taking some files across to the Secretary of State. When they arrived, the Contessina invited them both to supper. Holstein accepted with the usual proviso that there should be no other guests. Bülow greeted Phili in his patriarchal way, perhaps a shade more frigidly than usual, and drew him aside into a small private study. Then he carefully closed the door.

It was ugly news that greeted Philip Eulenburg. Bülow showed him letters, addressed to himself and to Hohenlohe, accusing Phili of unnatural relationships ; the accusation was supported by names and dates going back particularly to the Munich days, while Eulenburg was still Secretary to the Prussian Embassy.

Philip Eulenburg was furious. The slander could only emanate from Cuno Rantzau, Bismarck's son-in-law, whom he had at that time superseded in Munich. But if Rantzau was in it, then so was Bismarck, and Harden would be sure to hear of it, for he was hand in glove with Friedrichsruh. An accusation of this sort— whether false or true—would be a deadly weapon in Harden's hands, for he made his living by ruining people's reputations.

In consternation Phili asked what was to be done.

Bülow's reply was :

" Be a little more cautious, Phili."

Augusto, the butler, announced that supper was ready.

After supper the lady of the house sat down to the piano. She flung back the flowing lace at her wrists with a gesture that repudiated the mundane and the sordid. She played Liszt and Brahms. It was not hard to see who had been her masters. Holstein's thoughts wandered off. The music did not interest him. But towards the close one tune caught his ear. There was something about it that reminded him of the loveliest melodies of his boyhood, the old German popular songs, the only music that could stir his Prussian blood. He asked what sort of a song that was. Bülow replied not without a touch of superiority :

" Don't you know ? Why, that is one of the most beautiful of Phili's *Songs of the Rose !* "

Just then the voice at the piano began to sing :

*My darling stepped forth from my neighbour's door!*

Holstein was deeply moved. He begged for the song again. Then he rose and offered his hand, with unconcealed emotion, to Philip Eulenburg:

"Forgive me, Phili. I never dreamt you had written anything so lovely!"

## 47

# A FAITHFUL SERVANT OF WILLIAM I.

BISMARCK was dead. The news spread like wildfire through the whole of Germany. Friend and foe, at one in their grief, stood beside the bier of Germany's hero.

The Emperor wished the interment to take place in the Cathedral of Berlin. The funeral decorations for the interior of the cathedral were already being planned when the refusal of the honour came from Friedrichsruh. Bismarck had asked to be buried in his Saxon Forest.

Everyone who counted, pilgrimaged to Friedrichsruh for the last solemnities : the Emperor, the Chancellor, Bernhard von Bülow, and, of course, Philip Eulenburg. Geheimrat von Holstein alone remained in Berlin.

In the Nibelungen story the wounds of the dead hero begin to bleed afresh when the sinister form of Hagen draws near the bier. Holstein feared himself, and feared, even in death, his sometime friend.

On the station platform, Phili, always at the mercy of his emotions, and under their influence always inclined to be melodramatic, stepped with open arms towards Herbert Bismarck; but in full view of all, Cuno Rantzau's brother-in-law abruptly and pointedly turned his back.

Bülow saw the little scene and hung back; only when Herbert accosted him did he hold out his hand.

Holstein exacted a minutely detailed account of the proceedings, down to the epitaph which the old Imperial Chancellor had ordered to be inscribed in granite:

" Otto von Bismarck, faithful servant of William I."

It breathed loyalty to the past, endorsement of the Had-been, repudiation of the About-to-be— not many words—but each in granite. Old Bismarck had been true to himself to the last. Holstein took from a drawer the portrait of his former Chief, given to him years before, for years forgotten. "*Quand même !* " Henceforth Bismarck stood on his writing table beside the great Prussian King. No third portrait ever joined that company.

## 48

## "HOFFMANN!"

THE Emperor was at his hunting lodge, Hubertusstock. Bülow was in attendance. He had taken two books with him: Fontane's "Wanderings in the Mark" and Holtze's "History of Brandenburg." He studied both with minute care in order to be able to bring them to His Majesty's attention during an afternoon walk by the Lake of Werbellin. The Kaiser was naturally delighted to find how well read his Bülow was. The lives and doings of the old Margraves of Brandenburg had a peculiar interest for him at the moment, for he was just creating the Siegesallee in Berlin. Bülow turned the favourable opportunity to account, to broach the subject of Holstein's right to send private cypher telegrams. But here for once he had misjudged his man. The Emperor refused to interfere, on the ground that it would deeply offend "excellent Holstein." He would leave the Secretary of State and the Geheimrat to arrive themselves at an amicable adjustment.

"Besides," the Emperor added, "I am going to make Philip Eulenburg a Wirklicher Geheimer

Rat * with the title of Excellency. He is my best friend. I can however scarcely confer this title on him without conferring it also on Holstein. I authorise you to announce this promotion and the new title to Holstein on my behalf. That will give you a favourable opening."

When Bülow came to Holstein to convey the news his reception was damping :

" When I hear that a boot-licking painter fellow like Anton von Werner † is also to be an Excellency. . . . What use is the title to me ! I have toiled and moiled for forty years, and now I must try to look pleased that an artist who bedazzles His Majesty with effeminate Byzantine allegories is put in the same category as I am. Such a thing would have been impossible in the old days ! "

Bülow tried to assure him that His Majesty considered his services absolutely indispensable, that he recognised him to be invaluable as a diplomatist, and that he himself had been sincerely rejoiced over Holstein's elevation. As for the painter, Anton von Werner, to whom Holstein had alluded, he was recognised as an artist of quite outstanding achievement. Holstein would not admit it, he thought Werner as horrible as Begas ‡ ; Menzel was the only artist he had any opinion of. Finally, painting was not in his line.

---

* A higher title than Geheimrat.
† Court Painter to Kaiser William II., famous for his handling of historical subjects.
‡ Reinhold Begas, sculptor. Many of his statues and monuments are to be seen in Berlin.

The whole tone of this conversation irritated Bülow and made him raise the private telegram question brusquely. Holstein listened in perfect silence. When Bülow ceased speaking the Geheimrat got up, went to the door and closed it. Then the torrent broke loose. Bülow had never seen him in such a passion.

" Is it for this I lifted you above the common herd ! You would like to make me powerless. That might be all very well for you ! But, my dear Bülow, it must be one thing or the other ! Either you work with me or against me. If against, then one or other of us must go under."

" Very good," said Bülow with decision. " His Majesty shall decide. Now kindly let me out."

Holstein went to open the door. As he did so, he passed quite close to Bülow :

" And don't forget, at the same time, to tell His Majesty all about Mr. ' Hoffmann.' "

## 49

## FROM VERKI TO BERLIN

GENERAL VON WALDERSEE had conveyed to His Majesty the request of the whole body of generals that the Kaiser should graciously assume the rank of a Field Marshal in the German Army. The invitation was almost forced from them, since the Tsar and the Emperor of Austria had appointed the Kaiser Field Marshal in the Russian and Austrian armies, knowing that this kind of honour was especially welcome to William II.

The Kaiser joyfully accepted the invitation of his loyal army, and in his pleasure forgot his grievance against Waldersee. The Foreign Office still had files going back to earlier days which contained acid marginal notes about the General in the Imperial hand. Holstein betook himself to the Keeper of the Archives, and bade him take these papers round to Bülow so that he might see from the marginalia how His Majesty's feelings towards Waldersee had altered. Holstein meant this for a warning to Bülow not to get into too intimate relations with Waldersee.

The Emperor's favour, however, continued, and when the Boxer Rising broke out in the summer of 1900 he sent for the General to Cassel, met him himself at the railway station and seated him on his right hand. That evening he appointed Waldersee "General Field Marshal." The Kaiser took it as a matter of course that this man should lead the contingents of all the powers in China, since the German Army was the best and strongest in Europe.

Holstein groaned aloud, for it fell to him (against his own inner conviction) to convince the various ambassadors that it would be best to put Waldersee—ere long nicknamed the " World Marshal " —in command of the landing forces. The first to acquiesce was the Tsar. But Holstein did not attach very much importance to this success. He said to Bülow :

" The Kaiser has got an idea that when he and the Tsar agree, the entire globe will roll along in their wake ! "

In the end all the Powers agreed, the French last of all, ungraciously.

Waldersee reached China on September 27th. Pekin had been captured on August 15th. He had arrived too late.

While the Cassel conversation with Waldersee had been in progress, Prince Hohenlohe was far away in Russia, hunting wild boar in the Forest of Verki. A chasseur from Berlin found him in a shooting lodge. The messenger brought news that troops had been sent to China. Hohenlohe had been very indulgent, very patient—but this was too much. He betook himself to Berlin and handed in his resignation.

The chief candidates for the vacant post were : Philip Eulenburg, Bülow, Podbielski, Hohenlohe-Langenburg and Wedel-Piesdorf. The Kaiser would have preferred Phili, but even he had doubts whether his favourite would have the strength and staying-power necessary for the Chancellorship.

Holstein moved about from one group to another like a film-producer, calming one down, egging another on, in the faith of Bismarck's motto : "When the servants fall out the master is well served."

When everyone was reduced to complete bewilderment, Holstein announced that Bülow was the only possibility.

It was the morning of the 16th October, 1900. Frederick, the secretary, burst into the Bülow breakfast room and addressed the Foreign Secretary :

"His Majesty is telephoning from Homburg and wishes to speak to you, sir."

Bülow returned radiant from the telephone, answering his wife's enquiring glance with one word, "Yes."

Under this date in her Diary the Countess made an entry. The words are from Dante's *Inferno* :

*Quel giorno più non vi leggemmo avante !* *

Prince Hohenlohe spent his last evening in Berlin at Frau von Lebbin's. She had dressed herself in black for the occasion; the black woollen frock was closed right up to the neck so that she looked almost like an Egeria.

Prince Hohenlohe talked philosophically about the recent past. She sought to comfort him :

" But your Highness has accomplished wonders in these difficult times, that must be a consolation ! "

Whereat the Chancellor turned his beautiful eyes on her—eyes which his grandchildren still spoke of with enthusiastic admiration :

" Accomplished ?    Accomplished ?—Not a thing !  But hindered much ! "

* In its leaves that day we read no more.—(Cary.)

# IV. BÜLOW [1900—1909]

## 50

# GHOSTS AND VISIONS

ON the whole, the appointment of Count Bernhard von Bülow as Imperial Chancellor gave general satisfaction. A cordial letter of Herbert's brought congratulations even from Friedrichsruh. He could not wholly repress his hatred of Fritz von Holstein, and therefore strongly advised his friend to get rid of "all intriguers." He also proposed Radowitz as Secretary of State, for he knew that would make Holstein resign, since he and Radowitz hated each other like cat and dog. Only one person was a little sad about the Chancellorship, and that was Phili. If he was not equal to it himself, he would have liked to see it given to Prince Hohenlohe-Langenburg, for this would have left the Governor-Generalship of Alsace-Lorraine vacant, and that was a post he coveted for himself.

Bülow chose the alert, competent Richthofen as Secretary of State for Foreign Affairs, and the trustworthy von Mühlberg as Under Secretary. These appointments were made only after long-drawn discussions with Holstein, who, to tell the truth, did not approve of anybody, not even of these two.

Meantime, Waldersee had entered Pekin. The Boer War had flared up again. There was so much excitement and disturbance everywhere that cypher telegrams were continuously pouring in.

Geheimrat Willisch was in charge of the cypher office. He was a first-rate hard-working man; his only failing was that he belonged to some eccentric religious sect or other and was always having presentiments or seeing visions. About this time he told Holstein that the Day of Judgment was at hand and he had seen angels with trumpets riding white horses.

He had no sooner gone than Phili turned up in a great state of excitement. He had attended a séance on the Semmiring and had seen dreadful sights. Amongst other things Liebenberg on fire. His horror was redoubled when he found a telegram awaiting him in the Metternichgasse saying that Liebenberg was actually burning. He was on his way there now in all haste.

Holstein let him pour it all out and then said drily:

" Wait a moment ! "

He sank for a few seconds into intensive brooding. Then in an uncanny voice he announced to Phili :

" I'll tell you what is on fire at your place. The big shed behind the park. I'll tell you who was the witness when they set fire to it—your coachman, Grunwald. And I'll tell you who committed the arson, Heinz, son of the smith at Liebenberg."

Eulenburg felt all creepy. "For heaven's sake where did you get all these curious inspirations? I didn't know that you too——"

Holstein smiled: "The whole thing was in the *Kreuzzeitung* this morning!"

## 51

## A NEW FÜRST

WHEN Philip Eulenburg got back to Berlin from Liebenberg, Bülow took him aside and told him that he had been glancing through the confidential files reserved for the Chancellor's eye only. Amongst these were the ultra-confidential files about the individual diplomats. He had there found the report of an attempt by a bath-proprietor to blackmail Philip Eulenburg, attested by the President of the Police and countersigned by Hohenlohe.

Phili was furious. He wanted to challenge everyone all round. He would never rest till this mean intrigue was exposed. He would first go straight to the Kaiser and beg to be relieved of all his offices till this slander was proved baseless.

"If you do that, Phili, you wreck me. I should have to answer for betraying official secrets and that would be the end of me. You can see what it would involve."

But Phili was neither to hold nor to bind. He was so excited that he stormed out and left Bülow gasping. The Chancellor sent messengers to all possible hotels, restaurants and acquaintances to restrain Phili from any folly.

No one could find him anywhere.

Meanwhile, Philip Eulenburg was in bed writing a letter a mile long to Bülow. After long and calm deliberation he had decided to hold his tongue for the sake of old friendship, but he must say that he was getting weary of having any dealings with the sort of swine people were, and he thought of retiring. After that he started playing patience.

In the Palace everyone was waiting for the indispensable Phili. His Majesty had planned something to give him pleasure. When he still failed to appear an adjutant was sent out expressly to find him, for the Kaiser could not wait another moment for the "surprise." It was evening before the adjutant tracked Phili down : in bed at home. Philip Eulenburg, in his nightgown, took receipt of the Imperial letter.

On the envelope, decorated with the large capital W and the Imperial crown, stood the address, and Eulenburg gazed at it in surprise— like Piccolomini at the end of the play—" To Fürst Philip zu Eulenburg and Hertefeld."

## 52

## BÜLOW AS PUPPET

FRAU KYPKE was sitting in the Café Capça in the Calea Victoriei, Bucharest, with her friend Kiderlen. She was complaining, as often before, of the treatment she met with in official quarters, even in Bucharest; that her existence was systematically ignored, that people did not even greet her in public, that Bülow, for instance, ostentatiously ignored her in his letters. Whereupon she poured forth a flood of abuse about the Chancellor, maintaining, amongst other things, that he was as great a humbug and a liar as his wife, and that while he had his love affairs behind her back, she was equally unfaithful to him and carried on several amours with other people, including Lenbach.

Kiderlen smilingly puffed his Brazilian cigar. Here in Capça he was able to get his favourite cigars and his old Bordeaux, and here in his little private room he had found the only spot in this small Balkan town where he could live more or less in European style. He smiled at his friend's violent language, knowing that in her delicate position as his mistress she had a good deal to put up with.

But Kiderlen did not share her opinions and quietly corrected her in his easy-going way with a strong Swabian accent:

"Talking of Bülow, he has usually treated you with courtesy. It's not easy for him to do much at the moment. Whether he deceives his wife or not, I can't say, but I don't believe it. That she is unfaithful to him is common knowledge of the whole town, but that's none of our business. The gossip about the Taussig letters must not be taken seriously. If it were true that Holstein had got hold of them and wanted to use them for blackmail, Bülow could at once have taken proceedings. He would not perhaps cut a very dignified figure as a husband if the whole case came into court, but it would be the end of Holstein. He would be damned as a blackmailer. Whether Bülow has or has not men friends with whom his relations are unnatural, is an open question. Some people in Berlin speak openly about it, notably General von Hahnke. But Bülow is far too cautious to be caught out. He would never put his reputation at another person's mercy, least of all at Holstein's. If the Geheimrat in any way has got wind of things like this it may give him a pull behind the scenes. But he cannot turn it openly to account.

"There is a lot of oracular talk about Bülow's dependence on Holstein. I can tell you exactly how far it really goes. Holstein does all the spade work. Bülow is only a hollow shell. Holstein needs a façade of some sort to cover his work, for he is quite impossible in public. Publicity would embarrass him unspeakably, and public speaking was never his strong suit. The pair of them have shrewdly made a tacit compact, in which each makes good the other's deficiencies. Holstein stands for serious, well thought-out policies deliberately pursued. Bülow is concerned only for his personal position, the successful carrying out of his social duties, which he takes very seriously, the careful cultivation of his relations with the Kaiser and the Reichstag, the preparation of his speeches, which are either inspired by Holstein or written by Hammann— Hammann has done all his best ones for him— the granting of eternal interviews, and, finally, making sure that the Press duly pays homage to himself and his achievements. All this can only be attended to if a confederate behind the scenes gets on with the real work, and no one else could play the rôle so self-effacingly as Holstein ! "

While Kiderlen and Frau Kypke were thus entertaining each other in the Café Capça, an Imperial aide-de-camp in uniform was sitting in the waiting-room of the Foreign Office. The Geheimrat let him wait. At last an attendant ventured to insinuate himself round the door and begged leave to call His Excellency's attention to the fact that the Colonel had come round on His Imperial Majesty's business.

Holstein knew quite well what it was all about. This very morning he had handed in his tenth and penultimate resignation, this time direct to His Majesty. He wanted to ascertain just how high his stock stood in the Kaiser's reckoning.

The Imperial aide had brought the assurance of a very high quotation: His Majesty's portrait with a dedication—the highest favour the Emperor could bestow.

The Geheimrat took the photograph and pushed it into the drawer with all the others. And there it lay till his heirs unearthed it after his death.

## 53

## THE EMPRESS ATTENDS A
## PARADE

THERE was a great parade in Berlin on the Tempelhofer Feld in honour of the visit of the Shah of Persia.

The Emperor insisted on the Empress attending. Her carriage, driven *à la Daumont* with four horses and two postilions, drew up on the edge of the ground reserved for the March Past. She was wearing a white, tight-fitting dress and the orange sash of the Black Eagle; a black picture hat with drooping white feathers sat a little crookedly on her head. Her hair was already showing slight signs of grey. Beside the Kaiserin was seated her Mistress of the Household, Countess Brockdorff, dressed in silver grey; on the back seat Fräulein von Gersdorff, in an unbecoming mauve get-up.

" How lovely the Dragoon Guards look! I adore the blue and silver of their uniforms ! " exclaimed the Empress as the regiment rode by at a short trot. " I think it's the handsomest uniform in the Army. I almost envy Alexandra her lovely regiment ! "

The Empress had not observed that an officer on horseback had halted beside her carriage.

A sudden movement of her lace parasol caused the horse to shy, but the rider kept his seat gracefully : it was Count Bernhard von Bülow in the uniform of the Royal Hussars.

When he announced himself, he noticed that the Empress's manner was strained and distraught as she thanked him for his courtesy in coming to wait on her. He knew what was at the bottom of her distress : the constant friction between her and the Kaiser which Phili did all in his power to stimulate so as to be able to monopolise His Majesty.

" He will hardly succeed in the long run," thought Bülow, " for the Emperor is a trusty and faithful husband and his married life is an example to his people."

It seemed as if the Empress had divined the other's thought, for she volunteered :

" Eulenburg is not at the Parade to-day ! If he had come I should have had to stay at home. You'll have heard already that the Emperor has made him a Fürst. There are *others* to whom *I* should have given the title first ! " The implied flattery was not lost on Bülow. The Empress went on : " Otherwise I am always very glad to see our Protestant nobles being made Fürsts to counterbalance the Catholic nobility. In Uncle Chlodwig's * time we saw round us almost more

* The mother of the Kaiserin, Auguste Viktoria, had been Princess Adelaide of Hohenlohe-Langenburg before her marriage to Duke Frederick VIII. of Schleswig-Holstein-Sonderburg-Augustenburg, hence the Empress's relationship to Hohenlohe.

Catholic * Knights of Malta than Protestant Knights of St. John. There wasn't much to choose between us and the Apostolic Court at Vienna."

Bülow strove to change the subject. He told of other appointments which His Majesty was going to announce after the Parade. " Holstein is to be included. Jacobi has just told us that he is to be given the oak leaf of the Red Eagle."

" He must be a most competent official," said the Empress. " Please congratulate him from me ! The Kaiser has a very high opinion of him. It is only a pity that we never see him."

" A few weeks ago," answered the Count, laughing, " they were acting a play of the Irishman, Oscar Wilde, in Paris. It is called *Salome*. In it one of the Nazarenes says : ' He is everywhere, but it is not easy to find him.' It is just the same with His Excellency Fritz von Holstein." He laughed and saluted, taking his leave as the bugle-call " Officers ! " rang out over the parade ground.

" Always quotations ! " said the Empress as soon as the cloud of dust had settled behind the Chancellor.

" And quotations from a most blasphemous play ! " added Countess Brockdorff indignantly. " Dryander † has told me all about it and pointed the pitfalls of the subject out to me."

* Prince Chlodwig von Hohenlohe-Schillingsfürst was a Roman Catholic.
† Dr. Dryander, Chief Court Chaplain.

"They say Salome dances before Herod with nothing on at all," interjected Fräulein von Gersdorff. "Bülow doesn't seem to be a very good Christian."

"Oh, we mustn't go so far as that, my dear Gersdorff," protested the Empress, closing her parasol and giving the chasseur the signal for return. "We must remember 'judge not' in this case, too."

"Far be it from me, indeed, your Majesty to judge anyone," said the Brockdorff, "but it does seem to me a blasphemy to apply to Holstein the prophecy of the Nazarene. Holstein isn't a god."

"Perhaps he is, for Bülow," smiled the Empress a little sardonically, "but more likely a devil."

## 54

## A CAB AT THE TEMPELHOFER
## FELD

AMONGST many cabs drawn up on the other side of the Tempelhofer Feld, by the Barracks of the " Garde du Train " *—as it was jestingly called—was one which sheltered Holstein and Hatzfeld. The Geheimrat could have had for the asking a card admitting him to the more fashionable side, but he preferred not to risk going where someone might accost him !

Holstein had on his usual clothes, black trousers, black frock coat with waistcoat to match. His waistcoat buttons were covered in black cloth. He possessed two suits of this description, one for working in, and one for going to Borchardt's and for other occasions. He never kept a dress suit †—neither a dinner jacket nor tails.

Two overcoats and two hats completed his entire wardrobe. The hats were very old and very battered, and always recalled the stories

* The Tempelhofer Feld is flanked on the west by a number of barracks, behind which runs the railway and near which is a large military railway station.

† Correct ceremonial wear for day as well as evening functions.

about Frederick the Great, who was said to get his bodyguard to sit on his three-cornered hats to knock them into shape.

The two friends were well matched in their distrust and suspicion, and even in their positive prejudices they were mutually congenial.

Hatzfeld was justly accounted a very finished diplomat with a sure eye for realities. He now displayed his acumen as he retailed to Holstein Lord Salisbury's genuine hate and his determination to hem Germany in. The Ambassador faithfully reported the relations between France and England, which appeared to be growing closer and closer, so that France no longer troubled to make any secret of her desire for *revanche*. With all this Holstein was cordially in agreement. They also discussed most unreservedly the feelings existing between " Uncle Bertie " * and William II. The family relationship was more hindrance than help. Relations with Russia were entirely unfavourable. The Russian people gave no thought to Germany, and the Tsar was not allowing himself to be taken in by the Kaiser's clumsy overtures. The Emperor, in his annoyance, dubbed Cousin Nicky " a silly ass " (Jammerhuhn), which pretty phrase was, of course, duly reported. Hatzfeld had been the first to detect the danger of encirclement. Every one of his letters was full of serious warnings which unfortunately were scarcely heeded by

* Albert Edward, Prince of Wales, later Edward VII.

Bülow. Only yesterday the Chancellor had said to Holstein :

" The existing groupings cannot be altered all in a hurry. We must take these things calmly ! "

When Hatzfeld heard this phrase, he exclaimed :

" That is dilettantism *in excelsis !* "

Holstein implored him not to talk so loud, but the precaution was hardly necessary, for they were surrounded by a good-humoured Berlin crowd who were jesting away as they washed down their sandwiches with beer.

The burst of music that heralded the march off roused them from their talk. The glittering column yonder began to move. The Kaiser, with his magnificent suite, led the van, the helmet of the Garde du Corps with its flying eagle on his head.

" What a hullabaloo and display for one old Musulman ! " groaned Hatzfeld.

" Yes, indeed," Holstein agreed, " and last week when the Bismarck memorial was being unveiled the Emperor very pointedly wore undress uniform ! "

## ON RADOLIN'S BEHALF

THE German Ambassador in Paris, Fürst Münster, was eighty. He must be replaced; and various candidates were suggested who would worthily fill the post. Holstein proposed : Radolin.

As long as his friends remained friends they could reckon on Holstein's loyalty and good faith. In this case he sat down at once and wrote to Bülow :

"I have never yet asked a favour of you. Now I come with an urgent request. I have one good friend, only one—Radolin. Get him made Ambassador in Paris. If not for his sake, then for mine. I was already a Geheimrat when you were only a young attaché. Now you are Imperial Chancellor and I am still Geheimrat. I want neither promotion nor decoration for myself; do this for my friend ! "

" Characteristic, isn't it ? " said Bülow, handing the letter across to his friend and confidant, Geheimrat von Renvers : " I know the Spectre. When he gets sentimental he is more dangerous than ever ! "

## A NIGHT ADVENTURE

GENERAL DIETRICH HÜLSEN had become Chief of the Military Cabinet. This carried with it the doubtful privilege of being able to read the confidential file about himself. He found, amongst other things, a report by his former chief, Philip Eulenburg, written in his own hand, which turned the then military attaché Hülsen into a figure of fun. " This young man will never be able adequately to fill a post in Vienna, if only because his Berlin jargon sounds absolutely absurd. His wife would be equally out of place, and would be merely a laughing-stock in society on the banks of the Danube."

Small wonder that Hülsen hated Philip. Eulenburg, however, heard of this hate and did his best to assuage it. Phili knew that Hülsen's brother was anxious to become Intendant General of a theatre, so he persuaded the Emperor to make George Hülsen Manager of the Court Opera in Berlin. To achieve this Count Hochberg must first be sacrificed. He could only be got rid of if irregularities could be discovered in the management of the Court Theatre, for which his subordinate Hofrat Pierson was responsible. Philip Eulenburg therefore accused Pierson to the Kaiser of being guilty of interested intrigues and financial malversations. The unhappy man appealed in his despair to his chief, Count Hochberg, who promised to stand by him and enlisted Richard Dohna in the cause. Dohna, however, was the very man who had earlier fallen foul of Phili. His grievance against him was that he had been the first to introduce Philip Eulenburg at Court and that Phili had then taken no further notice of him.

His Majesty demanded the evidence on which Phili's accusations against Pierson were based, which indirectly implicated Count Hochberg also. Eulenburg forthwith cited Frau Bach in Munich as a witness.

Meantime the whole affair had reached Holstein's ears. He saw that Phili had got himself deeply entangled and that it would be impossible for him to find a way out. He knew where to lay his hands on a protocol in which Philip Eulenburg was accused of having belonged to spiritualist circles in Munich. According to another protocol, Phili had emphatically denied the charge, and further denied having any acquaintance with the leader of these séances, Frau Bach. And now, in the Pierson case, he had called as his witness this very Frau Bach of Munich, all knowledge of whom he had solemnly disclaimed. Holstein's time had come. He sent for Phili.

What passed between them on that fateful day, the 16th of May, 1903, no one knows. It is certain that Holstein blackmailed Phili, demanded that he should resign from all diplomatic employment and keep in future at a distance from the Kaiser; otherwise the Geheimrat would place his information at the disposal of Hochberg, Pierson and Dohna. Pierson was intending in any case, so Holstein averred, to bring the whole matter into court.

Philip Eulenburg asked for twenty-four hours' respite.

That night Pierson died.

Phili's star was again in the ascendant. Nothing could have been more opportune than Pierson's death.

When the twenty-four hours were up he visited Holstein and said he had not the smallest intention of giving up the Diplomatic. Holstein turned his great eyes on him.

"Good. Then I must do my duty. The last kindness I can show you is to repeat my advice to you to hand in your resignation to the Emperor to-morrow. I'll make it as easy for you as I can. If Hochberg falls, you could be made Intendant General of the Court Theatre yourself. I should have nothing against that. And that would give full scope to your talents."

Phili shook his head.

" It's too late for that. George Hülsen has already been appointed. I intend to stay."

Then Holstein took a step nearer to his victim and hissed—" Then I shall break you—Krause ! "

Philip Eulenburg went as white as a sheet and fell back towards the door.

" I resign ; I resign," he cried, as he fled.

Holstein sat on at his desk pondering long over the new turn of affairs.

" Whom shall we send to Vienna ? The Emperor and Bülow will be certain to insist on Wedel, but that must not be allowed. Wedel fought against Prussia at Langensalza. Who can be sure that he may not again work against Prussia in Vienna ? "

He could not think of anyone wholly to his mind.

He strolled out into the Tiergarten, still under the spell of the evening's happenings.

It was a moonlit night. The dark tree trunks cast heavy shadows over the solitary figure. Suddenly he started. Between the trees he had caught sight of a face, deathly white, like the face of a corpse or a marble statue, and the features were those of Philip Eulenburg.

Was it a vision ? No, he felt perfectly calm and perfectly clear-headed, and yet that dead, white face was Phili's. Slowly he drew nearer ; it *was* he. He went close, his hands stretched

215

out to feel the body in the darkness. It was as cold as ice, he was clutching a stone. A statue to Philip Eulenburg in the Tiergarten—? He walked round to the other side into the Siegesallee. It was the Hermes behind the big monument of the Elector Frederick I. of Brandenburg. Under the Hermes the words were engraved : " Wend of the Ileburg." This was an ancestor of Phili's, and the Emperor had ordered the artist to give him the well-loved features of his friend.

IT was the anxious time of the Morocco crisis. Holstein was in favour of going as far as was at all possible, so as to keep France in her place. If war should ensue, the moment seemed on the whole not unfavourable. Schlieffen was reported to have said :

" We are not ' *archiprêts* ' it is true, but the others are not ' *prêts* ' at all, so better now than later, when it will be harder still to tear down the barriers that hem us in ! "

An actively war-like mood was certainly prevailing in military circles at the moment. The Casinos were all for an attack. Only the Kaiser was unwilling to be drawn into a clash of arms. He felt with Moltke II., who was said to have remarked :

" If we must attack, well and good—if not : still better ! "

But the French on their side were shouting for *Revanche*. Lecomte was said to have murmured to Radolin, confidentially, but firmly :

" Voulez vous la guerre ? Eh bien ! Vous l'aurez ! "

For the moment, however, Holstein was

thinking of some step that could be taken independent of the military—for whom he had no love. Not one soldier was ever reckoned amongst his friends. He had never worn uniform himself. He had no use for soldiers. He wrote to Frau von Lebbin during those critical days :

" We must keep the military out of it as long as possible."

Holstein's plan, which was to begin with the Emperor's visit to Tangiers, was only partially carried out. The Kaiser himself flatly refused to go any further with the theatrical farce. He clearly saw that such procedure brought rage and hate to boiling point in France without any equivalent advantage to Germany. When Holstein heard that his programme had been cut down he was so much enraged that he took to his bed with internal hæmorrhage. It was the complaint that killed him four years later.

From his bed he followed with the liveliest interest the articles in the French Press, all of which were full of bitterness against him. For the French rightly recognised him as the *spiritus rector* of the Morocco policy.

Delcassé alluded to Holstein by name in the Chamber when he was speaking of his opposite number in Germany.

Meantime, there were plenty of people in Berlin who recognised the Holstein-Bülow policy as dangerous. Kiderlen wrote at the time to his friend Frau von Kypke :

" Hohenlohe spoke to me once about Holstein and said : ' All questionable and unfortunate counsels emanate from Holstein ! ' And so it is now. I hear that Holstein is believed to have Count Tattenbach in reserve to give him a position beside the Kaiser, in case the visit to Tangiers falls through after all ! "

On the 6th of June, 1905, the wedding of the Crown Prince was celebrated with delirious pomp and ceremony in Berlin. Count Bernhard von Bülow was raised to the rank of Fürst. Holstein also reached the height of his success : his enemy Delcassé fell on the same day. Holstein had reached his zenith. He had won ! Drunk with success he failed to see, or forgot, that this giddy height had been too swiftly climbed. The ascent had been successfully accomplished, but the road home was barred—an abyss was yawning beneath the nation's feet. The future was dark and threatening.

## 58

LUNCH AND A DUCK SHOOT

HERBERT BISMARCK never lived to see this apparent success of Holstein's policy. Even on his death-bed he kept repeating how black Germany's future looked and that the Empire which his father had created would sooner or later be wrecked by Holstein.

Holstein's next move after the humiliation of France was an attempt to bring about a reconciliation with Russia. He therefore fully approved the Kaiser's wish to arrange a meeting with the Tsar somewhere among the Baltic Islands. He insisted that the Chancellor must most certainly accompany the Emperor. That was a *sine quâ non*. But he was unable to conjecture what Bülow had up his sleeve, nor could he ascertain any details of the plans for the proposed journey.

He got the usual invitation to a *déjeuner dînatoire* at the Chancellor's. He took pains to ascertain who was going to be present. His Majesty had already accepted. It was to be an intimate party—*en petit comité*. The idea of feeding with the Kaiser at the Bülows' table seemed to Holstein perfectly fantastic. He tried all sorts of roundabout ways to find out all about everything without having to go himself. Walking through the Foreign Office garden he met Fürstin Maria Bülow. She immediately realised that for once he was inclined to accept her invitation. When he raised the inevitable problem of suitable clothes as a real deterrent she said, laughing :

" Come just in whatever kit you please, my dear Holstein. I'll undertake to make it all right with the Kaiser. You know His Majesty is really most anxious to meet you."

Whenever the Emperor accepted an invitation the list of expected guests had to be submitted to the Adjutant of the day. When the Kaiser saw Holstein's name he thought at first that there must be some mistake. He at once got into communication with the Chancellor and was assured that Holstein did indeed propose to come, unless that unaccountable person changed his mind at the last moment.

The Fürstin was busy arranging orchids from her hothouse on the round table. The flowers were inserted in glasses in a metal trellis. When she came to Holstein's place she gave the framework a little bend towards him, for she knew how short-sighted her guest was.

At one o'clock His Majesty's carriage drove up. Holstein was in the hall dressed in his usual frock coat.* The Kaiser stepped quickly up to him.

* What we call " evening dress " used to be the correct thing in Germany for ceremonial functions, even in the forenoon or afternoon.

After seventeen years on the throne he was for the first time meeting the moving spirit of his foreign politics. He admitted later that his first impressions were not favourable. Probably the old frock coat had something to say to that. How elegantly turned out the Chancellor appeared by contrast! Bending forward slightly he mounted the stairs always half behind the Emperor, so that his head just reached the knob of the Imperial dagger.

The Fürstin, always the perfect *grande dame*, was standing at the top of the stairs and accepted the Kaiser's kiss on her hand with inimitable grace. They proceeded at once to table.

The Kaiser was very lively during lunch. He spoke of the cordial telegrams the Tsar had sent welcoming the idea of a meeting, and suggesting Björkö, a remote island off the coast of Finland, as the rendezvous.

To Holstein's great amazement the Emperor declared that he would make this journey on his own and would not command the Chancellor's attendance. He would only take Tschirschky with him. The Tsar also wanted the meeting to be a private one and was leaving Lamsdorff in St. Petersburg and bringing only one representative of his Foreign Office.

Holstein drank in every word, watching the Kaiser narrowly and pondering over exactly what he would say to His Majesty when he was drawn into personal conversation after lunch.

They left the table and adjourned to the Fürstin's drawing-room. The Emperor stood still in front of a portrait of Donna Laura Minghetti, for whom he had a genuine admiration. Only a few weeks before he had with his own hand drafted a telegram to her announcing her daughter's new title of Fürstin. He talked about the Minghettis, about Rome, about the Palazzo Caffarelli, about the Villa Malta and the Villas Falconieri and Frascati. Holstein dutifully waited to be addressed.

" Bülow, where is that dachshund of yours ? " And Augusto had to be despatched to fetch Waldi. Then the Kaiser began comparing him with his own dachshunds. " Your beast looks so well-behaved, Bülow ! Mine are the terror of the house. They tear everything to bits : curtains, cushions ; why, they don't even spare the Adjutants' trousers ! "

The Chancellor laughed. Holstein was in despair. At last the Emperor turned to him :

" Well, my dear Holstein, I am delighted to meet you at last. You come from Schwedt, I hear. You must have known Goltz there—a good fellow, Goltz. I don't believe I ever had better duck shooting than I got there. Do you know those wild duck of the fens ? Now that really is a most interesting form of duck shooting, especially just after harvest. There are hundreds of them in the marshes along the Oder. I bagged forty-five in one day. It is the best of all duck shooting, I can assure you—far superior to what you get at Pless or at Donaueschingen or even in England."

The old Geheimrat stood silent. Mechanically he bowed and shook hands. The motor horns sounded from below. They seemed to call " Now here, now there." Holstein set words of his own to the same tune. They were :

" How I hate you ! "

## 59

## A CLOSED DOOR

IT is easy to see why the Kaiser hesitated to draw Holstein into a political discussion just then. He was always easily repelled by a shabby exterior. His half-English education made him attach great importance to a good tailor. It is quite possible that he felt so strong an antipathy that he could not at the moment bring himself to engage in serious talk with Holstein on this occasion. It is also possible, and more likely the real clue to his conduct, that he feared the man, and did not want to lay bare his own weaknesses. So he avoided the risk, by talking of—ducks.

The Treaty of Björkö is now seen to have been of comparatively little value. Tschirschky sanctioned the Russian addition of the words *en Europe* which neutralised the whole value of the treaty ; for a Russian attack on Persia or Afghanistan would have been the most serious possible menace to England. Holstein was bitterly disappointed and made no lack of covert criticisms and reproaches against Tschirschky. These were to bring forth evil fruit in their season.

The Secretary of State, von Richthofen, died on the 19th of January, 1906. Bülow, being in all matters of personnel entirely in Holstein's hands, proposed Mühlberg as his successor. Holstein would not hear of him. Next Bülow named Kiderlen. Holstein's shrewd comment was :

" There is room enough for me in the Foreign Office and doubtless there would be room for Kiderlen ; but there is not room for both of us ! "

This compliment to Kiderlen's quality endorses the Emperor's opinion :

" Kiderlen has the best brains in my Diplomatic Service."

Holstein had never been on particularly good terms with Kiderlen. The only taste the two had in common was good food and good red wine. This had often brought them together at Borchardt's, but Holstein could not endure Kiderlen's slovenly ways and he had a horror of his Swabian accent. Since Kiderlen insisted on living with his mistress, Frau Kypke, in what he called a " marriage of conscience," and wished to see her treated in every respect as a lady, the difficulty was always cropping up of how he and this inconvenient appendage could be suitably employed.

The Geheimrat at once detected the danger that Kiderlen might be allowed to replace not only Richthofen, but also Holstein. He was afraid to tender another resignation, so some other method had to be tried. Through somebody's indiscretion Holstein had got wind of compromising letters that Kiderlen had written to his mistress. In these he had indulged in some merriment about the Empress and the bourgeois life of the Imperial couple. The Geheimrat knew that the Empress had stigmatised Kiderlen as a "loose-liver." Here obviously he had a fulcrum for his lever. He induced an intermediary to lay before the Empress copies of these indiscreet letters of Kiderlen's and copies of some letters received by him, in the margin of which he had written "excellent!" beside certain passages. One of these contained the remark :

"With such a helmsman (as Bülow) and with the Kaiser as Captain the German barque is bound to find itself among the breakers!"

This ingenious plan was successful.

The Kaiserin, who rarely or never took a hand in politics, was tempted by this personal provocation, and lodged a request that Kiderlen "along with his mistress" might be left in Bucharest—a suitable place for him. The Court of Berlin would be better without him!

So Kiderlen was dropped and—a possibility Holstein had not foreseen—Tschirschky was made Secretary of State.

The Foreign Secretary's office adjoined Holstein's and the two had a communicating door.

On the first Tuesday after Tschirschky had taken office Holstein brought in some files. The new Secretary of State started; he had not expected His Excellency the Spectre to appear from this quarter.

" Put the files down ! I'll send for you when I want you ! "

No one had ever ventured to address Holstein before in words like these. Tschirschky forthwith turned the key in the door and explained the point of this manœuvre.

" You won't mind, your Excellency, coming round by the corridor in future ? I should prefer it."

When Frau von Tschirschky came that evening to fetch her husband from the office, he related the little incident :

" I couldn't work in peace for a second if I had the feeling all the time that at any moment Holstein might be standing behind my chair and looking over my shoulder with those uncanny eyes of his ! "

## 60

### BÜLOW FAINTS

THE Treaty of Algeciras was to be signed by the Great Powers on the 7th of April, 1907. France had not obtained all she had claimed in 1905, neither Protectorate nor Army; Germany, on the other hand, had secured freedom of trade in Morocco and a voice in the future fate of this dangerous corner of the Mediterranean.

Yet there were voices enough in Germany, especially in military circles, who talked of a " disgrace," and complained that " the honour of the nation " had not been upheld. There were many who would have welcomed an outbreak of war. The Kaiser did not share these views. He was not entirely satisfied with the tame conclusion of the lengthy Moroccan negotiations, but he preferred it to the arbitrament of war.

The Reichstag met two days before the actual signature of the agreement which terminated the Algeciras Conference. It was Bülow's business to justify the treaty to the people's representatives. The moderate parties were meek and signified their approval. But after Bülow, with his usual eloquence, had emphasised the difficulties of the negotiations and qualified the issue as favourable, August Bebel leapt to his feet. During his attack on the Imperial Chancellor's policy Bülow suddenly slipped from his seat in a dead faint.

Great excitement in the House! Geheimrat Hammann telephoned to the Fürstin, who feared the worst when she arrived to find her husband still lying unconscious in the Chancellor's tiny office at the Reichstag. As soon as Renvers, the physician in ordinary, arrived on the scene, he was able to reassure her : the attack was quite a slight one. The members of the Bülow block, who had been waiting outside for news, betook themselves in great relief to the refectory. The unfortunate occurrence was still the subject of lively discussion, a large group surrounded Bebel, whose attack had possibly brought on the seizure. Bebel was preparing to go in and make his apologies when Liebknecht, who could not endure Bülow, chipped in :

" You chaps may say what you like. I can tell you what's behind the fainting. The actor staged it intentionally. Why? That we'll find out before long."

## 61

## " . . . AND TSCHIRSCHKY LAUGHS "

HOLSTEIN was enraged. He marched gloomily down the corridors of the Foreign Office and muttered to his intimates :

" Never would Bismarck have put his name to a treaty like this ! "

The real reason of his annoyance was that they had made no use of his memorandum at Algeciras, but had worked on Radowitz's, Radowitz being Ambassador in Madrid and representative of the German Foreign Office at the Morocco Conference.

" Radowitz shall pay for this."

Holstein never forgave a man who had cut him out.

On the 1st of April, 1906, he had handed in his resignation ; the eleventh—and last. He knew that Bülow had read it and did not intend to let it go forward. The Geheimrat had no real intention of retiring, but he wanted to bring pressure to bear on the Chancellor and to emphasise his own importance. He had not reckoned on the fainting fit ; it was not on the agenda.

With Bülow's man Augusto, he scoured the whole house, like Bartolo in the *Barber of Seville*, to retrieve the document of resignation. The Chancellery messengers were pressed into the service and all hunted up and down till late into the night. Then Augusto solemnly declared that high or low it was nowhere to be found in the Chancellor's quarters. Holstein was well-nigh desperate.

The Fürstin had taken immediate steps after her husband's attack, to ask Tschirschky to take charge of all the official papers on the Chancellor's desk. He had done so. No wonder Holstein's search was fruitless.

Without hesitation Tschirschky handed on Holstein's tender of resignation to His Majesty, and strongly recommended its acceptance. He had the noose round the Spectre's neck. He drew it tight with a cold-blooded laugh.

In this curious way Fritz von Holstein made his exit from the Foreign Office after nearly fifty years of service. The brilliants of the Order of the Red Eagle were added to the other junk in the familiar drawer.

V. OUT OF OFFICE [1906—1909]

## 62

## YET ANOTHER DUEL

THE admission of Philip Eulenburg to the Order of the Black Eagle happened roughly to coincide in date with the acceptance of Holstein's resignation. Distrustful as ever, Holstein saw in this a proof that his fall had been engineered by Phili.

The historian Schiemann called on the Geheimrat on the 29th of April. In the course of his ingenuous conversation he mentioned that he had been shown the library at Liebenberg, which was kept in the most meticulous order. There was a collection of files there, the like of which he had never before seen in a private person's house. He had made a haphazard choice of one file case and found documents in it with which he supposed even the Chancellor was very likely unacquainted.

Holstein took fright.

Something must be done to put Phili *hors de combat*.

On May 1st he addressed a letter to him which begins :

" My Phili ! This form of address is not intended as a token of esteem, for ' Phili ' amongst our contemporaries denotes — well — nothing good. You have now attained the object you have for many years pursued—my removal. The current Press attacks must be exactly to your liking!"

Then follow extracts from the notes he had made for his own private archives. Their unambiguity is perfect.

Philip Eulenburg had no option but to send a challenge, naming the Ambassador to Württemberg, Baron Axel Varnbühler, as his second. Holstein chose as his the retired Ambassador, von Derenthal. The terms on which the duel was to be fought were exceptionally severe: distance, ten paces, with freedom to advance. Drawn pistols. Exchange of shots till disablement or death.

The two seconds spent days trying to reach acceptable terms for a reconciliation. Finally, Phili drew up a long declaration, the climax of which was that he had never worked for Holstein's fall and that he had never had part or lot in Press attacks on him. Holstein then withdrew his letter of April 1st. Bülow gave his final blessing to the reconciliation and the record of the episode was filed in the Foreign Office.

Some days later the Keeper of the Archives was to register the document. It was nowhere to be found. Geheimrat von Holstein had induced some third party to purloin it. It was safely housed in his iron safe in the Grossbeerenstrasse. He needed it!

## 63

# HARDEN AND HOLSTEIN

IN everyday life Holstein was wont to use arresting phrases which were not normally current, and which are not readily forgotten. The expression " think thrice," for instance, was one of his favourites. In the *Zukunft* of the 8th of December, 1906, Phili read the words " that he (Harden) would think thrice before he would accuse any man of maintaining relations with Fürst Philip Eulenburg ! "

Holstein was, in fact, now acting as Harden's prompter. Attacks against " The Round Table of Liebenberg," against Philip Eulenburg and his friend Kuno Moltke, Commandant of Berlin, became daily more frequent and more definite. The coterie was openly accused of Spiritism, Faith-healing and other morbid tendencies. The paper would not attach importance to these manifestations in themselves, were it not that they occurred in circles unfortunately frequented by the Ruler of the German nation.

Two men intervened to try to silence Harden. Walter Rathenau and Baron Berger, Director of the German Theatre in Hamburg. Those in favour of bringing matters to a head so that light and order might prevail were Lucanus, Hülsen and, more especially, General von Plessen. The two former were members of the Emperor's Cabinet and Hülsen was actuated by the hate provoked by Phili's reports against him in the old days at Vienna. General von Plessen had the whole of the Maison Militaire behind him.

The spirits of Liebenberg sank. Kuno Moltke, who was the most bitterly attacked, saw nothing for it but to take an action against Harden.

The news was in the evening papers. Frau von Lebbin read it aloud to Holstein, who by this time was almost blind. He was elated. The battle had begun. " Kuno Moltke is the first act, Philip Eulenburg will be the second, and the aim of the third will be the removal of the Kaiser."

Bülow understood the full significance of the news. He shared Lichtenberg's philosophy : " The fly that would escape swotting is wise to settle on the flap." Harden was the fly-flap. Bernhard von Bülow forthwith took refuge in the enemy camp.

## 64

### REHEARSAL

H ARDEN'S fight against "The Camarilla" was widely taken up. A journalist named Brand declared that the Chancellor Bülow was "one of them," thus accusing him of the same perversities as Moltke and Philip Eulenburg. The Chancellor prosecuted. The case was to be heard in Moabit.*

Holstein had of course no longer any official status, but he continued privately to advise Bülow. The Chancellor naturally did not want to advertise his continued connection with the Geheimrat, so he gave him instructions to come in through the garden from the Königgrätzer Strasse and up the iron stair. Confidential servants who could be trusted to hold their tongues would be there to show him in.

One September afternoon in 1907 Holstein wanted a talk with the Chancellor and came without appointment. Just as he was putting his foot on the first step of the spiral stair, he heard Bülow's voice coming from a ground-floor room which did duty as a large office. The door was

* A suburb of Old Berlin with a Criminal Court and a Prison.

only partially closed. Holstein glanced in and stopped in amazement. The whole room had been cleared. Two reading desks had been erected. At the one stood Hammann in the rôle of Public Prosecutor, at the other Hofrat Müller, representing the President of the Court. Bülow was moving about between the two. It was the rehearsal for the prosecution of Brand.

Again and again they went back to the beginning.

"Bülow, the actor, is practising his part!" thought Holstein. "But why all these theatricals when he need only be perfectly natural?"

First the Chancellor got ready for his entry, then with elastic steps he traced a slightly curved route up to Müller's desk; a smile, a greeting to Müller, then to Hammann, a slight bow to the dais, no further greeting, but a little gesture; then marked dignity; the witness's oath; the deposition obviously learnt by heart (and checked by Hammann from a manuscript draft on his desk); the close, the bow as before; dignified exit. When he had practised it all and got it word-perfect and found everything tally to his liking, he caught sight of Holstein. For a moment he looked embarrassed, then he took the Geheimrat's arm and led him up the back stair.

At the top he buttonholed him:

"I was just going to ask you a favour! Would you be good enough to come with me to-morrow? It would make a good impression if you would confirm my deposition. I have no one who knows me as well as you—you will have long since forgotten unpleasant little brushes in the past—you must stand by me to-morrow!"

Holstein watched Bülow's fingers nervously toying with the buttons of his coat. He turned his eyes full on him and hesitatingly refused :

"Lena and I are just off to the Grunewald to-morrow to enjoy this lovely autumn weather. I can't easily back out of it!"

Nevertheless, Bülow's triumph on the morrow was complete. The judges even rose from their seats as the Chancellor left the Court. Brand was given the maximum sentence of eighteen months' imprisonment.

## 65

## BALLET AT DONAUESCHINGEN

ON the 28th of October, 1908, the *Daily Telegraph* printed a long article with the headlines : " The German Emperor and England. Personal Interview. Frank Statement of World Policy. Proofs of Friendship." The article was prefaced by the words : " We have received the following communication from a source of such unimpeachable authority that we can without hesitation commend the obvious message which it conveys to the attention of the public."

The authority was Colonel Stuart Wortley (retired) of High Cliff Castle, Isle of Wight, whose guest the Emperor had been after the Cowes Regatta. While staying at the Castle the Kaiser had aroused the most lively and friendly interest among his host's friends by expounding his views on England.

Sir Cecil Spring Rice said about this time : " The prevailing opinion in English circles is roughly this : ' An understanding with the Kaiser himself might very well be possible ; an understanding with Bülow is out of the question, because we don't trust him.' "

So the Emperor's outspokenness seemed an admirable opportunity to influence public opinion in England in favour of Germany. The Kaiser gave his consent to the publication of the interview, stipulating only that it should first be submitted to the Chancellor and the Foreign Office so that they might make, beforehand, any comments they wished.

The Emperor went to his shooting estate at Rominten and from there this interview was sent to Klehmet, Councillor of Legation, who sent it on to the Chancellor in Nordeney. Bülow did not read the manuscript—whether intentionally or unintentionally—and it got into print in its original form.

The effect in England was electrical.

In the interview the Kaiser stated, amongst other things, that he had drawn up the plan of campaign against the Boers, or at least that the plan Lord Roberts adopted was the same as the one he had sketched. The House of Commons inquired whether any such plan of the Kaiser's existed in the archives of the War Office. The reply was an emphatic denial. General laughter in the House. The effect in England was lamentable. But the storm raged even more fiercely in Germany.

Bülow, having taken counsel with Holstein, worked for nights with Hammann and Löbell—Holstein lashing up hostility against the Kaiser the while—drawing up explanations, corrections,

R 2

counter articles, to mitigate the phraseology of the Imperial indiscretions. The Reichstag staged a debate to prevent the recurrence of a similar episode. Bülow implored the Emperor to stay in Berlin and weather the crisis, and not, whatever else he did, to set off on fresh travels.

The whole temper of Germany was bitterly hostile. Ballin wired from Hamburg that if the Kaiser attempted to visit the town there would certainly be demonstrations against him. The Conservatives were the loudest in protest. They saw the whole monarchy tottering. Holstein was more active amongst them than anywhere. He would have liked to crown his life work by compelling the Kaiser to abdicate. The news that the Emperor was in fact toying with thoughts of abdication only spurred him on to renewed attacks. The moment had come to plot for a change of monarch.

The Emperor disliked unpleasantness and longed to escape from the insults that were being heaped upon his innocent head, to fly to friends who would help him to live through these trying times, so he inquired whether he might visit the Fürstenbergs at Donaueschingen. With the invitation to come, he received also the welcome news that his friend, the Archduke Francis Ferdinand, was there, too. With his full suite he therefore set out for the Black Forest.

Bülow was in despair. This made all personal reports impossible and in a time of crisis all business would have to be laboriously transacted in writing. Holstein was morosely sinister. He had one aim left in life : to annihilate " the two noxious mischief-makers, the Kaiser and Philip Eulenburg."

While the statesmen in Berlin were at their wits' end evolving some scheme to end the crisis, Donaueschingen was busy organising festivities to charm away the Emperor's low spirits. The 14th of November, 1908, was fixed for a Cabaret festival. The host, Prince Fürstenberg, and the entire Imperial party were assembled in a big hall where the various items of the programme were to be produced. The last was to be the climax of the evening—the solo dance of a ballerina. The lady to take the part was no less a personage than the Chief of the Military Cabinet, General Dietrich von Hülsen.

He danced in a little skirt of tulle which left his body naked from the waist up and his great legs bare.

Enthusiastic applause. A profound curtsy. The ballet-girl flung one more flower at the Ruler's feet, then danced with lightly tripping step backwards to the door : and behind it, collapsed. General von Hülsen, aged fifty-six, Chief of the Military Cabinet, Imperial Wing-Adjutant, had danced himself to death.

This did not help to raise the spirits of Donaueschingen.

## 66

## DOWNFALL OF PHILIP
## EULENBURG

HOLSTEIN was not destined to see the fall of the Emperor whom he hated, but he was granted the triumph of Phili's utter disgrace. His tool Harden was not wont to do things by halves.

As the Kuno Moltke case dragged to its close, everyone perceived that this was only the *lever de rideau* to a new and larger and more sensational scandal, the prosecution of a member of an ancient noble house, a Knight of the Order of the Black Eagle, Fürst Philip zu Eulenburg-Hertefeld, intimate friend of the Emperor.

He was compelled to take oath. He solemnly swore that he had never been guilty of moral perversities. Harden retorted with an accusation of perjury, adducing evidence that the Fürst had, for instance, indulged in unnatural relations with fishermen of the Lake of Starnberg. A revolting inquisition by Harden into the private life of his victim followed, based, unfortunately, in part on Holstein's portfolio. The Crown Prince kept the Emperor *au courant* and the Kaiser withdrew in horror from his sometime friend. Bülow had long since deserted him. Philip Eulenburg, already an aging man, no longer physically able adequately to defend himself, stood deserted before the court of law, subjected to the crossfire of lawyers and of Harden's witnesses. The tried and trusty friend of the Emperor was dragged from one court to another by his persecutors, while the hostile pack rejoiced in his disgrace. They were insatiable. The persecution and the tally-ho went on even after Holstein's death, until the quarry perished of exhaustion in utter loneliness.

## 67

## A FAREWELL VISIT

ASENSE of insecurity permeated the whole
of Berlin society. The Kuno Moltke,
and Harden *versus* Eulenburg cases offered
a warning. Even the Kaiser had lost some of his
self-assurance. The first time that he spoke in
Berlin after the *Daily Telegraph* affair he read his
speech painstakingly from the written sheet.
This was unprecedented.

The Chancellor felt none too secure either, and
talked of resigning—not very seriously, it is true.
For him the worst thing was that Holstein was
ill, seriously ill, so that there was no hope of his
ever coming back. With him, Bülow had lost
his mainstay. Kiderlen had been impressed into
the Foreign Office, but he was not a colleague
of the same type as the self-effacing Holstein.
Kiderlen was ambitious.

The Bülows went to see Holstein on the 27th
of April, 1909. As they drove down behind the
Belle-Alliance Platz and into the neighbourhood
of the barracks of the Dragoon Guards they were
both very conscious of the change of atmosphere.
This was still the real Berlin—not the artificial
civilisation of the Wilhelmstrasse and the Linden.

In Holstein's modest living-room they found a friend of theirs, Frau von Lebbin. She was sitting with a glass of tea in front of her and eating sandwiches which she had brought with her for Holstein and herself.

Before showing the visitors into Holstein's bedroom she warned them how ill the patient looked. In spite of this preparation, the Chancellor was horrified to see how yellow the invalid's complexion was, and how terribly his cheeks had fallen in. The Fürstin handed him some lily of the valley she had brought, and sat down in an armchair beside the iron safe which had become nearly as legendary as His Excellency the Spectre himself. Bülow remained beside the bed.

Holstein spoke very slowly. He warned his friend more than once against the Russians, who would not be likely to sit down under the annexation of Bosnia and Herzegovina; he urged the need of standing by Austria-Hungary. The Chancellor listened attentively to Holstein's earnest admonitions about politics ; he felt these warnings and counsels were probably the last he would ever hear. Once Holstein smiled almost cynically—it was when Bülow mentioned that he was now working with Kiderlen. A book was lying on the table beside the bed. Frau von Lebbin had been reading aloud to the invalid. It was in French, a language Holstein loved and of which he was a master. The Fürstin enquired the name of it. " ' Les Mémoires du Prince de Ligne, Maréchal de France.' One phrase in it fits my present case exactly : ' Man arrives at the grave-side at last, as a dreamer at his own hall-door.' "

When they were out in the street again, Bülow said to his wife :

" Did you notice Bismarck's photograph on his writing table ? Holstein is an amazing fellow. He hated the old man. And yet. . . . They say after all that hate is only an inverted form of love. When I think of the pair of them, I often remember a saying that seems to hit Holstein off : ' What is spiritual and true in the thought of the master often becomes false and material in the mouth of the disciple.' "

## 68

### HOLSTEIN DIES

WHILE Bülow was discussing Bismarck and Holstein with his wife, Holstein was making comparisons to Frau von Lebbin between Bismarck and Bülow.

" The two have nothing but the initial in common," he said. " Bülow has a good head, but Bismarck had a great soul. Bülow talks people over, Bismarck convinced them. Bülow is cleverer and more subtle, but Bismarck thought his own thoughts, while Bülow only pirates those of other people and twists them with amazing skill to his own purposes. Bülow's policy is ruthless. I see that too late! I haven't the strength to hold him in any longer. Now that I can look back over the whole, I think that there has never been so double-dyed a hypocrite as Bülow since the time of Cæsar Borgia. He reminds me of a rocket that sizzles and dazzles and finally— stinks! Isvolski said to me once that Bülow had reduced flattery to a system. That is strictly true!"

On the 6th of May the pain grew more acute. A neighbouring doctor was called in. The patient had a temperature of 101°. Next day it was up to 104°. No one called. Frau von

Lebbin and the suburban doctor were alone with the dying man. The fever became worse in the night. Left unguarded for a moment, he got up and tried to reach the safe. Suddenly Frau von Lebbin heard a cry. She dashed into the room and found her patient on the floor. He had pulled a curtain down with him in his fall. He tried to speak, but she could not understand him. He pointed to the outline of the safe and groaned:

" There he is ! There ! Arnim ! "

And he fell to trembling.

They fetched the doctor and got the sick man back to bed. They took down the curtains and put a screen in front of the safe and rearranged the light so that he should not see into the corner. The whole night he tossed in delirium.

Towards morning he grew less restless. Then he asked for his prayer book, the one he was given long ago in Schwedt for his confirmation. Two women had gone to Church with him that day—his mother and his sister. To-day two women stood by his death-bed, Lena Lebbin and Röberchen his faithful housekeeper. He begged his friend to read him his favourite hymn " Commit thou all thy griefs. . . . " *

He tried to fold his hands in prayer. Frau Röber helped him. It was the 8th of May, 1909.

Fritz von Holstein died at the age of seventy-two.

* Gerhardt's well-known hymn : Befiehl Du Deine Wege . . (translated by John Wesley).

## 69

### THE OBITUARIES

THE Berlin newspapers printed obituaries with large headlines. The *Berliner Tageblatt's* closed with the words : " Holstein was wholeheartedly a man, a rarity in an age when half measures pass muster as statecraft ! " The *Strassburger Post* meant much the same thing when it said : " It is incontrovertible that Holstein was one of the most competent and most experienced diplomats whom Germany has ever possessed ! " The *Vossische Zeitung* pertinently wrote : " A whole cycle of legends has gathered round his personality, and posterity will find it even more difficult than his contemporaries already do to distinguish the fact from the myth."

Harden, the professional detractor, devoted the front pages of the *Zukunft* to Holstein. Amidst his protestations of friendship he left nothing unsaid, except the fact that Holstein had used him as a tool, and that in doing so he had classed him with all other Jews, of whom he was wont to say, " Use them ? Yes : but reluctantly."

The foreign Press also did justice to Holstein's memory. The *Temps* of the 9th of May wrote : " We must not, in the moment of his passing,

omit to pay a due tribute of homage to this
enemy of France. Few men had greater knowledge, few laboured more eagerly, passionately,
for the greatness of their country, few depised so
heartily as he the flashy rewards of personal
success. His pride was in loftier things." The
English *Daily Mail* said of him : " He was the
prototype of the Prussian official of the old
school." And Kiderlen, whom the Emperor
called " the rising man," said truly : " A faithful
friend to his few friends ! A dangerous enemy
to his many enemies ! "

When his executors came to put his affairs in
order they found nothing except his meagre
wardrobe and his modest personal effects. The
sole object of real value was the diamond star of
the Red Eagle, and that Frau von Lebbin handed
back to the State.

## 70

## THE FUNERAL

THE humble funeral took place on the 10th of May. The man who for more than forty years had been the controlling spirit in German foreign policy was carried to his grave unaccompanied by any representative of the Emperor.

The mourners were few.

Faithful Radolin set out from Paris immediately on receipt of the news. When he opened his newspaper next morning in Cologne he read that the Kaiser did not propose to send either a representative or a wreath. Faithful Radolin, who owed everything to Holstein, took fright and hied him in all haste back to Paris.

On the other hand, one mourner was present whom no one had expected and whose attendance caused surprise amongst the rest : the Ambassador Radowitz. Holstein had waged war against him all his life, and had never missed an opportunity of injuring him. Evil tongues were not lacking to start the rumour that Radowitz had come only to assure himself that the coffin was really buried deep enough and that His Excellency the Spectre would never " walk " again.

The modest cortège wended its way to the Invaliden Cemetery. The simple grave lies there in the Scharnhorst Strasse, covered to-day with ivy. A granite stone bears name and date :

FRITZ VON HOLSTEIN
Wirklicher Geheimer Rat
born 4th April 1837 at Schwedt on the Oder
died 8th May 1909 in Berlin.

If some curious visitor seeks out this peaceful cemetery in the midst of the bustle and noise of the metropolis, he will not easily find the grave. No one knows Holstein's name. Quickly men forget—and are forgotten. He rests under the trees between Scharnhorst and General Hoffmann. Here sleep the heroes of Prussia, and it is just that Fritz von Holstein should have his place amongst them, for his one passion was to make his country great.

After a long, toilsome and curious life, he is at rest.

# EPILOGUE

## EPILOGUE

Christmas Eve, 1914.　　On the Semmering.
Hall of the Hotel Panhaus.

His Excellency von Tschirschky and a small circle
of friends.

THE Ambassador took off his gold-rimmed
glasses and gazed in front of him a long
while before he spoke:

"If you ask me why I helped Holstein to his
fall I must answer because I thought him a baneful
man, a man who might have suited the Middle
Ages or the Renaissance, but who was not of our
time.

"He always wore the mask of a conspirator.
He worked underground and shunned the light
of day, because he was too awkward to face the
public and was a bad speaker. I always thought
him morally shifty. He could not look you in
the face. He often seemed timorous and subser-
vient. His methods lent themselves to legend.
He seemed unearthly. I have never seen messengers or servants so intimidated, so terrified-
looking, as those who had to wait on Holstein.
They literally trembled before him and only dared
to speak in whispers.

" Nor was it only his subordinates whom he could paralyse with terror, but cultured men too. I have known thoughtful people like Radowitz and Pückler come out of his room in a sort of hypnotic trance.

" Now . . . having made these unkind remarks, I realise that I must in justice say something on the other side, too.

" The Geheimrat was unquestionably a terrific worker. You could bring him a pile of files in the morning, which another man would take a week to work through; Holstein would have them polished off by evening. And with it all his work was exemplary and scrupulously exact.

" His immense knowledge and incredible memory made him a walking encyclopædia, at the service of every responsible leader of Germany's foreign policy.

" Bismarck could read this book, at need could bang it or fling it at the wall. Caprivi could not dispense with the Compendium Holstein, while Hohenlohe just liked to flutter the pages now and then. Bülow was impotent without this magic primer, and so in his day Holstein became the real power behind the Foreign Office.

" A strong Chancellor could make brilliant use of Holstein's qualities, but under a vain and superficial man like Bülow they were dangerous.

" When I handed his resignation to the Kaiser in April, 1906, I was fulfilling a public duty and I knew it. The Foreign Office did not exist as a permanent hobby-horse for His ageing Excellency, and official tenders of resignation could not be allowed to become a farce. I got rid of him because I knew younger and better men to take his place.

" While I say this—and while the cannon in the Carpathians are thundering through the stillness of this holy night—I must face the question : ' How far does the guilt of this war rest with Holstein ? '

" I am now holding Philip Eulenburg's post of Ambassador in Vienna, and am still suffering from political blunders of Holstein's. His persevering and ostentatious support of Aehrenthal, for instance, prompted an anti-Russian policy in Austria. This led to the annexation of Bosnia and Herzegovina, and this again increased the Russians' hostility. This tension between Russia and Austria was the main problem of pre-war politics.

" There is an old hymn book in my family. One hymn in it begins : ' It is hard to be a Christian ' and on the next page stands one : ' It's not so hard to be a Christian . . .'

" It is much the same with Holstein. It is easy to judge him harshly, but it is not so easy to judge him fairly, for he undoubtedly had great qualities.

" The pros and cons will make his biographer's task a difficult one. The history of Holstein will be the history of a remarkable period in which the strange figure of Fritz von Holstein will neces-

sarily bulk large, for he represents a whole and
perfect type amongst a lot of half-baked contemporaries who could not evade him, and were
driven either to flattering him on the one hand
or to hating him on the other!"

# SELECTED BIBLIOGRAPHY FOR
# ENGLISH READERS

## HOLSTEIN AND HIS PERIOD

Bethmann-Hollweg. " Reflections on the World War,"
translated George Young, 1920 (Butterworth).

Bismarck. " Reflections and Reminiscences," 2 volumes,
translated F. A. J. Butler, 1898 (Smith & Elder).

Brandenburg, Erich. " From Bismarck to the World
War, 1870–1914," translated Annie Elizabeth Adams,
1933 (Oxford).

Bülow. " Imperial Germany," 1916 (Cassell).

Bülow. " Memoirs," 4 volumes, translated Voigt &
Dunlop, 1931–32 (Putnam).

Curtius. " Memoirs of Prince Hohenlohe-Schillingsfürst," 2 volumes, translated Chrystal, 1906 (Heine-
mann).

Eckardstein. " Ten Years at the Court of St. James's,"
translated George Young, 1921 (Butterworth).

Haldane, Viscount. " Before the War," 1920 (Cassell).

Haller, Johannes. " Prince Philip zu Eulenburg-Hertefeld," 2 volumes, translated Ethel Colburn Mayne,
1930 (Secker).

Hammann. " World Policy of Germany, 1890–1912,"
translated M. A. Huttman, 1927 (Allen & Unwin).

Headlam. " Bismarck," 1899 (Putnam).

Huldermann. " Albert Ballin," translated W. J. Eggers,
1922 (Cassell).

Lee, Sidney. " King Edward VII." 2 volumes, 1925
(Macmillan).

263

# BIBLIOGRAPHY

LICHNOWSKY. "Heading for the Abyss," translated Professor Sefton Delmer, 1928 (Constable).

LUDENDORFF. "My War Memoirs," 2 volumes, 1919 (Hutchinson).

LUDENDORFF. "The German General Staff," 2 volumes, translated F. A. Holt, 1920 (Hutchinson).

LUDWIG, EMIL. "Bismarck," translated E. & C. Paul, 1927 (Allen & Unwin).

LUDWIG, EMIL. "Kaiser William II.," translated E. C. Mayne, 1926 (Putnam).

NICOLSON, HAROLD. "Lord Carnock," 1930 (Constable).

"PLESS, DAISY PRINCESS OF." By Herself. Edited Chapman-Huston, 1928 (Murray).

ROBERTSON, CHARLES GRANT. "Bismarck," 1918 (Constable).

VON SCHOEN. "Memoirs of an Ambassador," translated Constance Vesey, 1922 (Allen & Unwin).

SAZONOV, SERGE. "Fateful Years," 1928 (Cape).

STRACHEY, LYTTON. "Queen Victoria," 1921 (Chatto & Windus).

TIRPITZ. "My Memoirs," 2 volumes, 1919 (Hurst & Blackett).

VICTORIA, QUEEN. "Letters, 1862–1901," edited G. E. Buckle, 1926–32 (Murray).

WHITTON, F. E. "Moltke," 1921 (Constable).

WILLIAM II. "My Memoirs, 1878–1918," 1922 (Cassell).

WILLIAM II. "My Early Life," 1926 (Methuen).

WILLIAM II. "The Kaiser's Letters to the Tsar," 1920 (Hodder & Stoughton).

WILLIAM, CROWN PRINCE. "I Seek the Truth," translated Ralph Butler, 1926 (Faber).

PRINTED IN GREAT BRITAIN BY THE WHITEFRIARS PRESS LTD.
LONDON AND TONBRIDGE